"Shelby Abbott has a sharp min
brings both to bear on some of t
churches today. He writes with the wisdom of a mentor but the tone
of an older brother who's on your side. This is a terrific resource with
so much biblical and practical guidance."

Sam Allberry, Speaker, Ravi Zacharias International
Ministries; author of *Seven Myths about Singleness*

"Being a student is stressful. We're at an age and time where pressure feels perpetual and overwhelming. So we need help. We need
resources from those who've been there and done that and can give
us seasoned, brilliant advice. Enter Shelby Abbott. Shelby's not only
been there and done that—he works full-time with students who are
still doing it. He's funny, biblical, faithful, and wise. *Pressure Points*
is a book every college student needs to read."

Jaquelle Crowe, Author of *This Changes Everything: How
the Gospel Transforms the Teen Years*

"*Pressure Points* serves as a timely book full of wisdom to transform
life's greatest pressures into opportunities for spiritual transformation. Shelby Abbott offers a beautifully written, vulnerable, and
biblically sound book to guide us on our journey through the stress
of finding purpose, managing relationships, and understanding suffering. With excellent discussion questions and relatable examples
to explore, you'll love reading this book alone or with a group. Don't
miss this book!"

Heather Holleman, Faculty Commons, Cru; author of *Chosen
for Christ: Stepping into the Life You've Been Missing* and *Seated
with Christ: Living Freely in a Culture of Comparison*

"Shelby's put together an excellent work. I know he says it's for college students, but I can't imagine anyone in any stage of life not feeling every one of these pressure points. He helps us see that so many
things that cause us stress in life don't have to be distractions that
take us away from Jesus, but they can be divine signposts—each
one highlighting a unique thirst for satisfaction in Christ. A must-
read for all students who will find themselves inevitably struggling
through these issues."

John Onwuchekwa, Lead Pastor, Cornerstone Church,
Atlanta, GA; council member, The Gospel Coalition

"The pressure of decisions, relationships, and failures can be overwhelming, yet God's Word supplies grace to calm our anxious hearts. *Pressure Points* applies God's truth to these stressful areas in a way that strengthens our faith in the God who promises to care for us every step of the way."

Garrett Kell, Lead Pastor, Del Ray Baptist Church, Alexandria, VA

"With children in grade school, high school, and college, my family is just now learning to navigate the stresses and strains of student life. My children are grappling with the unique challenges it brings and we, as their parents, are learning to lead them through it. *Pressure Points* is just the guide we needed to do this well."

Tim Challies, Blogger at www.challies.com

"When it comes to student ministry, there are few people I trust more than Shelby Abbott. I've watched him up close and far away. He understands the challenges, the struggles, and the angst that so often haunt the college years. In *Pressure Points: A Guide to Navigating Student Stress*, Shelby deftly blends biblical insight and experiential wisdom to help young people navigate life-shaping questions. Buy two copies of this book—one for that twentysomething in your life, and one for yourself. You won't regret it."

Matt Smethurst, Managing Editor of *The Gospel Coalition*; author of *1–2 Thessalonians: A 12-Week Study*

"Life grows increasingly complex, and adulting brings challenges we underestimate and don't expect. Shelby Abbott invites you to process tensions under the surface in your life while helping you practically navigate pathways to finding belonging, worth, meaningful relationships, and purpose."

David Robbins, President & CEO, Family Life

"Shelby nails it with *Pressure Points*. This book is a must-read for any Christian university student who walks passionately with Christ yet is honest enough to admit they struggle with the unique pressures that can trouble a young person at such a formative period of time as college."

Josh D. McDowell, Author and speaker

PRESSURE POINTS

A GUIDE TO NAVIGATING STUDENT STRESS

SHELBY ABBOTT

New
Growth
Press
WWW.NEWGROWTHPRESS.COM

New Growth Press, Greensboro, NC 27404
www.newgrowthpress.com
Copyright © 2019 by Shelby Abbott

Cover Design: Faceout Books, faceoutstudio.com
Interior Typesetting and eBook: Lisa Parnell, lparnell.com

ISBN: 978-1-948130-34-9 (Print)
ISBN: 978-1-948130-37-0 (eBook)

Library of Congress Cataloging-in-Publication Data

Printed in Canada

26 25 24 23 22 21 20 19   1 2 3 4 5

For Quinn and Hayden.

Contents

Foreword

I've heard things like this said many, many times and have even
said them myself.

"I am afraid that . . ."

"I just can't deal with the pressure."

"I know I shouldn't be, but I'm worried about this all the time."

"I didn't get much sleep last night, I guess I couldn't get
_____ out of my mind."

"I try to push _____ out of my mind, but I just can't."

"I'm dreading having to face _____."

"The thought of _____ just overwhelms me."

"I pray for peace, but I'm anxious."

If you haven't said these things aloud, you've probably whis-
pered them under your breath and if you haven't ever verbalized
them, you've most likely thought them. Why are these things the
universal experience of us all? Well, the answer is clear. Between
the "already" of our birth and the "not yet" of our death, God
has chosen for us to live in a world that is fundamentally broken,
not functioning the way that God intended. Because this is the
address that God has chosen for us, none of us will successfully

escape its brokenness. Inevitably, this brokenness will enter your door. I like the way this is explained in Romans 8. It says that the world we live in "groans, waiting for redemption." You groan when you're in pain, you groan when you're disappointed, you groan when you're overwhelmed, and you groan when the pressures and anxieties have gotten to you.

But there is more. The Bible teaches us, from cover to cover, that this brokenness is not just outside us, it's inside us. Since that terrible moment of disobedience in the Garden of Eden, humanity has been broken. Just like the world around us, we don't always function as God intended. We don't always think what we should think, desire what we should desire, choose what we should choose, speak as we should speak, or do what we should do. So, it's not just the physical world around us that groans, we too groan. You could argue that between the "already" and the "not yet," groaning is the default language of us all. If you listen to yourself, there is probably never a day when you don't groan about something, and if you listen to others, you will hear them groaning too.

You may be thinking, *Paul, this is not very encouraging. I think I'm too depressed to read the rest of this book!* But wait! Into this brokenness and groaning the Bible speaks the most beautiful message that you could ever hear. It's not a set of therapeutic strategies, a system of philosophical observations, or an abstract theology. It is a narrative—a story of how God has invaded our world of brokenness and personal struggle in the person of his Son, Jesus. It's about how he offers mercies that are new every day and form-fit for this particular moment of need. Jesus knows what you need because he, like you, walked the twisted and rocky paths that you now walk. He faced all the things you now face, so he responds to you with life-changing, hope-giving, and life-directing sympathy and understanding.

What gets me up in the morning is the knowledge that Jesus didn't just die for my past forgiveness (I'm so glad he did!) or for my future in eternity (I'm very grateful that's my destiny!), but also for everything I face in the here and now. He died for every hurtful relationship, he died for every personal failure, he died for every temptation, he died for your anxiety, he died for those over-whelming pressures. He did what he did for you so that you would have everything you need to be what you've been designed to be and so you could do what you've been called to do.

Think about what this means. God hasn't given you a self-help manual; no, he's given you a much more wonderful gift, the gift of himself. Which means that you are never alone in any situation, location, or relationship. He hears and understands your groaning and he offers you what you would never have if left on your own.

Now you may be wondering what this has to do with the book you have begun reading. I know the kind of book I want to read and I would suspect it's the kind you would want to read as well. First, I want a book that is honest about the things that all of us face. I don't want to read something that minimizes my experi-ence or denies the things I have to deal with. But I don't just want honesty: I need hope. I want the hope that offers me understand-ing, comfort, perspective, and direction. The Bible is shockingly honest and gloriously hopeful at the same time. The honesty doesn't crush the hope and the hope doesn't negate the honesty. I love that both of these things are in this book you're about to read, as well as the fact that neither is weakened by the other.

When I am looking for a book that addresses something I will face in my life, I ask four questions:

1. **Does the writer know the topic?** It won't take many pages for you to become convinced that Shelby has much more than a theoretical understanding of what this book is about. He knows from experience what pressure points are about and so he writes not like a seminar lec-turer, but like someone who has walked in your shoes.

2. **Does the author understand the audience being addressed?** One of the strengths of this wonderful book

is that Shelby has studied, listened to, ministered to, and lived with the audience that this book addresses. His descriptions of you and what you face will never seem inappropriate, awkward, or off-base. Because he cares about you, he has cared to know you, and that personal understanding adds power and integrity to what he has written.

3. **Is the author willing to be honest and transparent?** I love the fact that Shelby doesn't write like a person who thinks he has arrived. He doesn't stand above you and talk down to you. He writes as a fellow traveler who has walked where you walk, struggled where you struggle, has reached out for help like you do, and has discovered the only place to find real help—not just for him, but for you too.

4. **Does the writer have a street-level understanding of the gospel story?** This is what excites me most about this book. Shelby really does understand the rescuing and transforming power of the right-here, right-now grace of Jesus. He has a real grasp of the practical wisdom God's Word has to offer you. He understands we're not just meant to think the Bible's theology, but we're meant to live it as well, and when we do, good things result. And he knows that the gospel of Jesus Christ, when applied to your everyday life, has the power to change everything. For him, what Jesus did is not just about the past and the future, but also about everything you face right now.

So, I commend this book to you. It is worth the investment you are about to make because it embeds your story in the larger story of redemption, and because it does, it will offer you not only hope, but also help that really helps!

Paul David Tripp
September 26, 2018

Introduction

I've felt it before. The push applied to my little world that knocks my routine out of alignment and sends me reeling. Sometimes the push has been small and nagging, and other times it has been suffocating and overwhelming. I've encountered the push recently in the last few hours, and I can remember experiencing it all the way back when I was six years old.

It came once when I shaved my legs on stage in front of thirteen hundred college students simply for the purpose of entertaining a crowd (I won't elaborate on that at this time). It came once when my stepdad called me and told me my mom was being helicoptered to a hospital because she was in a life-threatening accident (she's fine now, by the way).

It came when I stood in a room holding a diamond ring with my heart pounding out of my chest as I waited for my future fiancée to come in and be surprised by my presence. And it came just a few months ago when my wife asked me to my face if I was lying to her about how much television I let our kids watch the night before while she was out.

The push is called "pressure," and I've felt it before. No doubt you've felt it too in your own life and know exactly what I'm talking about.

Maybe you call it by a different name, such as stress, hardship, trials, friction, tension, obstacles, difficulty, or challenges. But regardless of the title you ascribe to it, I'm certain you've experienced it. Sometimes it's pressure that leads to a joyous outcome, sense of accomplishment, or growth. Other times, however, it's pressure that leads to distress, heartache, darkness, or depression.

Regardless of the outcome, one thing is certain: pressure is present in everyone's life. Sure, it can come in all shapes and sizes, but pressure is inevitable. It's also polarizing, meaning that for the follower of Christ it will generally lead a person away from the status quo of everyday life and toward one of two places. One option is toward bitterness, anger, and resentment of God for what he has "done to us," and the other option is toward a richer understanding of Christ's life, spiritual growth, and union with God.

I have been in full-time Christian ministry working with young people like you for nearly two decades, and I've seen the kind of pressures you as a twenty-something can go through on a regular or even not-so-regular basis. And since I've been neck-deep in the issues of college students or young professionals in the context of ministry for many years, the pressure points have become easy to spot. This season of life is uniquely stress-filled, and perhaps even more so than any other life stage because of the amount of decision-making that takes place in such a short period of time. Your decisions as a college student can and will shape your future reality, making college time potentially the most stressful of pressure cookers.

In recent times, however, I've noticed different kinds of struggles bubbling to the surface in the lives of young men and women just like you who want to walk with Jesus. In many ways, the root hardships you face reflect the basic obstacles of many who have walked the path before them, but the pressure points today have taken on a new kind of variance that older generations have not had to deal with at all before.

Our modern age—saturated with technology, constant cynicism, streamlined digital communication, heavy negativity, relationship status posts, and instant information access—has shaped the way many young people deal with the pressure points of life. It has constructed a culture unlike anything we have ever seen or experienced—a culture that promises joyful connection via ever-present social networks, yet in reality is associated with depression, common mental problems, and socioemotional difficulties.[1]

In reality, the familiar everyday problems of older generations have mutated into a whole new set of issues because of the current culture's drastic influence. It's a real complexity that needs to be met with the weight of the only real solution. Namely, the gospel.

This book will be an intentional push toward the life-giving spirit who is Jesus Christ (1 Corinthians 15:45), because "our hope is built on nothing less than Jesus' blood and righteousness."[2] While our current crisis may appear to be new in nature, Scripture still has the best insight on how to deal with the inevitable pressure modernity thrusts upon us. Jesus Christ remains the same yesterday and today and forever (Hebrews 13:8), so the writing that follows in this book will take God at his word and apply the principles of Scripture to today's unique pressure points. My prayer is that you will be able to see the clear gospel solutions to our troubles in the modern age as you ask important questions like:

"What do I really believe?"
"How do my beliefs change the way I deal with the pressures of my day-to-day life?"
"Does knowing Jesus *really* make a difference in my life? If so, how?"

The Setup

For the sake of ease and clarity, I've separated this book into three main sections I believe thoroughly tackle what categories of life most weigh on you as a young person once high school ends and your new life begins: Purpose, Relationships, and Difficulty. Additionally, each chapter concludes with three reflection questions to help you think deeper on the topic and perhaps write out a few thoughts.

Within the three main sections, we'll talk about some of the specific pressure points where the "heat of life" is applied to your reality, and how we as followers of Jesus Christ can appropriately apply the gospel. The unique trials you face might initially tempt you to escape or default to your favorite coping mechanisms, but what I want you to discover is that life's pressures are not an inconvenience to be retreated from or sidestepped. They are a wide-open invitation from Jesus to draw near to him and connect with him in ways you may have never done before. Jesus says in John 16:33, "I have said these things to you, that in me you may have peace. In the world you will have tribulation. But take heart; I have overcome the world." Christ promises us difficulty (tribulation), and hardship should never come as a surprise to the believer because the Bible is filled with it. Yet in the midst of such trials, Jesus says that in him, we can have peace. Why? Because even though the world is filled with trouble, Christ has overcome the world.

This is such great news because it removes the burdens of life from our shoulders and pushes us to embrace the power of the gospel over its inferior substitutes we have a tendency to run toward. But first, let's make sure we're talking about the same thing here when we say the word "gospel."

What Is the Gospel?

All human beings think they know what is best for themselves, and that is why we are born to be rebels. All of us turn our backs on God and go our own way because we think we've got it all figured out. We substitute purity for poison and drink deeply from the unwashed cup it rests in.

And although we are condemned to separation from God because of our rebellion, he still chooses to move toward us by absorbing the deserved punishment himself in the person of Jesus Christ. The solution has presented itself quite clearly, and every person in the world is faced with a choice: personally receive the punishment for our own defiance, or let him do it. The price has to be paid.

Those who humble themselves and take the gift God offers become children of God, and they no longer bear the burden of condemnation (Romans 8:1). But the incredible reward God offers in Jesus is not just a ticket to glory; it is the beginning of a relationship unlike any other. It is a personal relationship with our Maker, built upon true love, trust, intimacy, tenderness, and care. Eternity with God begins the day we make the decision to receive what he has offered, and when we take it, he begins the good work of healing us from within. Then, and only then, are we able to live a life characterized by the gospel, because the foundation is solid.

Jesus is in the business of changing lives. He always has been, and he can do the good work of transforming you to be more like him, despite the run-ins you will undoubtedly have with life's pressure points. All you have to do is ask him to get involved and trust he'll follow through with his promises.

And he will.

This is the good news of the gospel that dramatically alters the way we view not only our eternal future but our present struggles as well. In the midst of the pressures that will inevitably come our way, we can choose to lean into Christ, the Prince of Peace (Isaiah 9:6) with power over sin and death (Romans 6:1–11), instead of fleeing toward the escapism of our vices.

I'm praying that my words in the form of this book will guide you well as a means of great encouragement. If you allow what is presented here to mold your perspective regarding the craziness of our modern environment, I think I'll be able to help turn your gaze toward Jesus, even as your phone buzzes in your pocket.

The Pressure of Finding Purpose

Many college students wonder, *What is my purpose in life?* And as you begin to draw conclusions to answer that question as a university student, you make decisions that begin to shape the look of your future. First you make your choices, then your choices make you. So asking the right questions about life and looking for the answers in the right place is key. Section 1 will guide you to ask the right questions when the pressure points hit, seek biblical answers, and help you understand your purpose.

1

Does God Even Like Me?

Back in college at the beginning of my sophomore year, I liked this girl named Katie. She was cute, funny, and fairly involved in our campus ministry, so we got to hang around each other quite a bit for the first couple months of that school year. Katie and I would often find ourselves pairing off at group gatherings to talk and get to know each other a bit more in the midst of the chaos that is the Christian collegiate social construct.

One such event was a group hangout at someone's apartment off campus, talking, snacking, and playing games until it got late. I remember talking with Katie at the party and sticking close to her as things wound down so I could walk her home to campus and get more time with her that evening.

Sure enough, after the hangout, I found myself sitting on a couch with Katie and another friend Anne, when Anne spoke up to the room and said, "Katie and I are gonna go. Would any man here like to walk us back to campus?"

I quickly volunteered to walk them both back, and after doing so in what I could only assume was an attempt to be funny, my friend Anne looked at Katie and said, "Does he count?"

Here's the thing—I'm short. I've always been that way, and from a very early age, I remember being made fun of for being below average when it came to height. Naturally, I joked about this on a regular basis to get laughs and protect myself from getting injured by the cruelty of people's words, should they be inclined to get laughs themselves at my expense. I would just try to beat them to the punch.

And because I was regularly willing to shell out short jokes about myself, Anne probably felt comfortable that night doing so, thinking it would be funny and really no big deal. What Anne didn't know, however, is that I would carry that little three-word question with me for years to come. It deeply wounded me and defined the heart of my struggle in life as a person, man, friend, romantic option for a girl, missionary, and even child of God.

Does he count?

For the longest time, I have struggled with that question, wondering in all seriousness if I was the kind of guy anyone was looking for on any particular, relational level. I remember asking myself questions like,

Does anyone really want to be friends with you?

Are you good enough to be a part of that group?

Why would a girl like her ever consider having feelings for a guy like you?

Why would God ever do something remarkable with someone like you?

The Bible says God loves you, but does he like you?

Do you count?

Inevitably, this line of thinking led to some fairly dark places, and the resulting insecurity made me think and act in ways I'm pretty embarrassed about when I examine my behavior as a young person. In other words, I overcompensated for my insecurity with constantly trying to be the goofy center of attention.

It wasn't until a mentor of mine looked me in the eye one day and asked, "Do you *truly* believe God isn't disappointed in you?

Do you really believe there is no condemnation for *you*, who is in Christ Jesus?"[1]

Of course, when he asked me those questions in the tone he did, I couldn't help but realize I was living with an anti-biblical mind-set about who I was in Christ. He was implying (and rather bluntly, I might add) that my day-to-day behavior would suggest I needed the approval of others to feel validated because I wasn't receiving my validation from the truth of God's Word. Upon deeper examination of my heart, his implications were correct.

I felt convicted about my attitude and behavior, so I turned to the Lord. Here were his words to me: "The Lord your God is in your midst, a mighty one who will save; he will rejoice over you with gladness; he will quiet you by his love; he will exult over you with loud singing" (Zephaniah 3:17).

Rejoicing over me with gladness and exulting (or joyfully celebrating) over me with loud singing told me quite clearly that God delights in me as his child. Nobody is joyfully singing about someone if she is simply tolerating that someone. You can't cheerfully celebrate people if you love them but don't like them. God's affection for me isn't something he begrudgingly checks off a list because he has to. His care and love for me is as clear and intentional as parents for their newborn child. Look at Psalm 149:4: "For the Lord takes pleasure in his people . . ."

If you were playing a group get-to-know-you game with a bunch of people and the question posed to you was, *What do you take pleasure in?*, your mind wouldn't go to things, events, or relationships you felt had to come out of your mouth. You'd immediately think of the people, things, or experiences that brought joy to you in the past, and a smile would no doubt come to your face.

This is the way God thinks and feels about us, his people. God takes pleasure in us. He delights in us. He celebrates and sings loudly, fawning over us, his precious children. God reminds us of his love all through the Bible (Psalm 147:11; Romans 2:29;

1 Corinthians 4:5; and 1 Peter 1:6–7). And once I realized this truth from the pages of Scripture, I began to realize how real it was that God delighted in me. I do count. He does like me. And he likes you too.

Jesus Is the Proof

I know that many of us have real reasons and real guilt that lead us to believe God might possibly not like us, but with a clear understanding of Scripture, we can see that's not true. The Bible points us to the gospel, and the gospel shows us that God does more than just tell us he loves us; he shows us as well. He proved his love to us when he sent his Son to this world. If you've ever wondered exactly how God feels about you, you'll find your answer in the life, death, and resurrection of Jesus Christ. Seriously. You never have to wonder how God feels about you, because he's already made his feelings abundantly clear through the words and actions of his Son made known through the Bible.

How much does God want to be in relationship with you? Well, he sent Jesus to live a life of suffering so you might benefit. He was attacked by people trying to kill him. He was misunderstood, rejected, and disrespected. He was unjustly condemned to a painful death, he was deserted by friends and even his God. The fire of God's wrath burned him to the core and blazed unchecked over him. He was utterly and entirely alone. And why? Because on the cross, Jesus was suffering not only *with* us but *for* us.[2] That's how much God wants to be near you. That's how much he's willing to sacrifice to get close to you and be in relationship with you. He plunged himself into the fire for you when he went to the cross, and all doubt about his feelings for you should end with the truth of the gospel. Jesus is the proof. Case closed.

So what exactly does this mean? It means you and I are free to live in the security of knowing how our Maker feels about us. We are not under the oppression of public or private opinion about who we are, what we look like, or how other people might treat us. We are fully known, loved, liked, accepted, and adored by our Father in Christ Jesus.

Counting the Likes

I have known many people who clamor for attention and acceptance both in person and on social media because they are clearly starving for the approval of others. It's almost as if every posted selfie and self-congratulatory humble brag online says to the world, "Please like me! Please validate me! Please think and comment about how beautiful, funny, sexy, or talented I am! Please give me worth!" We count the "likes," pore over the analytics, tally the views, add up the followers, and make an evaluation of who a person is based on the numbers.

This is just the status quo of our modern age. We're devastated when someone unfollows or unfriends us to the point that we wrap our value up in the sum total of individuals who may or may not want to look at what we post online every other hour. Today, unlike any other moment in human history, social media presence equals real world importance.

But this is not so with the God of the universe. In his eyes, you are not how many friends you have on Facebook. You are not the number of followers you have on Instagram. You are not the number of views or thumbs up per YouTube video post. He sees you for who you truly are, flaws and all, and still says, "Yes please."

"For our sake he made him to be sin who knew no sin, so that in him we might become the righteousness of God" (2 Corinthians 5:21).

Did you see that? Paul leads off in 2 Corinthians 5:21 with, "For our sake." God took all of our sin and placed it on Christ, making him into sin, and he took all of Christ's righteousness and placed it on us, making us pure. He performed this "great exchange" *for our sake.* He did it for us so we might know him and be close to him. This is what God thinks about you. He likes you!

If and only if we embrace the fact that God already embraces us, we will have the ability to snap out of the enchantment our social media feeds have on us. We won't rest our worth on the shaky ground of digital public opinion. We won't fight to gain and keep new followers as if our lives depended on it. We won't obsess over the perfect picture to post that will get the most likes, and we won't get downtrodden when the likes don't add up the way we would've assumed. Additionally, our drive for acceptance by others in the context of our real-world relationships too will dwindle in the face of God's affection.

In fact, it will be the way God intends for life to be. We will live contently in the warm embrace of the One who likes us no matter what, because the payment for his acceptance was made by the blood of Jesus Christ on the cross. That internal faith and security we hold will be reflected in all our interactions (in person or online), helping authentic followers of Jesus to stand out in bold contrast to a world that lives and dies by the like.

Does God Even Like Me?—Reflection Questions

1. Is there any anti-biblical viewpoint you hold concerning your self-opinion? If so, what is it?

2. How have you convinced yourself that God might love you, but he also just tolerates you? After reading passages like Zephaniah 3:17, how are you able to definitively say God loves you *and* likes you?

3. How have you been tempted to believe social media presence equals real-world importance? Be specific.

2

How Do I Decide My Life's Direction?

A few years ago, I was attending a conference with a bunch of college students, and the speaker on stage asked the crowd if anyone in the room had trouble with decision-making. A vast majority of the people in the room raised their hands, and then he asked if any over-analyzers were in the room. Again, a lot of hands went up, this time coupled with some nervous laughter. Finally the speaker asked if any of us had trouble making a decision about whether or not to raise our hand, and we all laughed.

I'll admit my hand went up when he asked about decision-making. I'm a huge over-analyzer. I mentally debate the pros and cons of both big and little decisions all the time because I want to make sure I'm making the best choice. And naturally, as a follower of Jesus Christ, I want my choices to fall in line nicely with God's will.

The angst of going against the Lord's will for my life has been a constant companion since the day I first said yes to Jesus. I've consistently battled creeping thoughts that I might be doing or saying or thinking something that might be displeasing to him, and that battle has made me nervous. No doubt you've probably had the same problem from time to time in your walk with God.

As Christians, we experience the unique struggle of wanting to please our King because we value more than just our own happiness. We value what he values, and if we begin to think for a moment that our values aren't in line with his, frustration can infiltrate our hearts and overtake us.

My goal in this chapter is to explore the biblical way to make decisions about our directions in life and to expose some inaccurate ways of thinking about why we do what we do. Living by faith means you can make decisions, depending on God, his words to you, and the help of others.

I Feel Called

To start, let's talk about the word "calling." It's probably fair to say Christians use the word liberally when it comes to conversations about decision-making and God's will.

"I believe God called me to apply for this job."

"I'm pretty sure God is calling me to text her back."

"I think God is calling me to leave this church."

"I'm feeling called to break up with you."

"I just really felt called to buy that new $90,000 sports car."

You get what I'm saying, right? Inevitably, you've mentioned that God has called you to something at some point in your Christian life to justify a certain decision. And while I'm somewhat poking fun right now at how Christians can abuse the term "calling," most of the time our hearts are probably in the right place when we say it. However, the Bible doesn't necessarily define the word in the same way we might define it, and we need to be careful about using the word as a blanket excuse for doing whatever we want while we tack God's name onto our own personal desires.

The Greek word for "call" (*kaleó*) is used 147 times in the New Testament,[1] and when it's used, most of the references have to do with our calling to salvation or toward sanctification. Very few times is it used in reference to purposeful functions or action-able calling, such as the specific how-tos of life. Therefore, we can clearly understand from the way it's predominantly used in Scrip-ture that our primary calling as Christians is to the lordship of Christ.

By means of God the Holy Spirit, he calls us to himself, and that irresistible *call* draws us into an eternal relationship with God the Father through the Son, Jesus Christ. Additionally, we are *called* to sanctification under God's lordship that we might become transformed into the image of Christ as we grow in our relationship with him (Romans 6:19, 22; 12:2; 2 Corinthians 3:18; 1 Thessalonians 4:3; 1 Peter 1:2). Salvation and sanctification define the lordship of Christ in our lives, and both involve God's authoritative rule in the life of a Christian.

God's rule over our lives should always be the main thing, and secondary to it is our calling to service. The subplot of our stories as believers is figuring out how to live on mission for Christ, and the subplot (by its own nature) should never trump our first prior-ity of a life in submission to God. As my mom used to say, "Never put the cart before the horse." Lordship drives how we serve, not the other way around.

Calling is different than what we might at first think. It's not a thing I do, per se, but really more of who I am. My calling is a reflection of my fundamental identity that comes from God and remains the same throughout my entire life. A calling is not the same as certain specific responsibilities, but more of the way my life is lived out in my church, my job, my connections, and my relationships. My life is a way I express my calling via my pas-sions, my giftedness, and the way God has wired me. My calling is not a specific task, but who I am in Christ.

When we understand that our calling is about who we are in Christ, this significantly changes the way we go about life in our culture today. The consistent worry about whether or not "I'm doing what I'm supposed to be doing" withers away in light of the fact that my call is to live under the authority of Jesus and to walk with him each day. As I spend time reading the Bible and meditating on its truths, I'm able to easily comprehend what it means to be refined by the power of the Holy Spirit, and I'm consequently able to rest in my salvation and sanctification instead of worrying about some specific "calling." There is no concern about the assurance of my salvation because I remember and think about Christ's work on the cross for me. There's no room for anxious wondering when I see that it is his responsibility to do the work in my heart to make me like him. Where "calling" perhaps used to carry with it a lot of baggage that made me believe I always had to get it right, an understanding of the true biblical definition helps me see that I can drop my baggage at the door.

This is especially important in light of our modern age. I've seen countless online posts in various formats from my Christian friends talking about calling and what the Lord has led them to in their decision-making. And therein lies my point. I've seen *so many* posts about what people feel the Lord is telling them to do, I've sometimes felt "out of the loop" as if I've missed some special revelation from God on what I should be doing in my day-to-day decisions. When I read all about what Jesus is telling my friends and family to do, the subtext for me is, "Uh, why am I not hearing from the Lord the way other people do? How are they so confident the Almighty has given them personal instruction when I can't even figure out what clothes to put on and what cereal to eat in the morning?"

The prevalence of social media and online instruction (either intended or unintended) can in many ways cause the average person to feel as though he is the only one who lacks God's contact information in his phone. When seemingly everyone around him has direct access to the will of God for their lives and he doesn't, confusion and frustration are never too far behind.

But we should all be cautious about what we label publicly as "calling" when it comes to our decision-making. Once we understand that it is less about the nitty-gritty of life and more about our new identity in Christ, we have a clear biblical awareness of the term and can use it correctly. To make the error of misusing our "calling" for all to see on social media and the like is to potentially cause our brothers and sisters to stumble.

There is true blessing in knowing your calling as a child of God. The Bible calls us to walk humbly with Christ, and as we do, it gives us confidence that all of our decisions large or small will be led by God's Spirit.

How Do I Decide My Life's Direction?
Reflection Questions

1. In what ways have you previously misused the word "calling" when it comes to your decision-making?

2. What do you think it means that Jesus is our Lord? If our calling is to the lordship of Jesus, what does lordship look like?

3. How has social media and Christian posting affected your view of God and his specific instruction in your life? Has it encouraged you or discouraged you?

3

What Does God Want Me to Do?

What is God's will for my life? That's a question that young people are constantly trying to figure out. They are wondering what to major in, who to date, how to spend their time, and what job to shoot for after graduation. With big life decisions comes speculation about what God wants for them, and how they should proceed. Along with the questions often comes fear—fear of the unknown and fear of making the wrong decision.

But finding out what God wants us to do in life has to begin with asking the right question, and *What is God's will for my life?* is simply the wrong question to ask. Since that is where most people start, let me explain what I mean.

Let's say you and I were trapped inside a house that was burning down, and I looked at you and asked, "Since it's getting hotter in here, do you think I should remove my jacket?" Now, the question itself is certainly relevant to the specific fact that because of the fire, the temperature is rising in the house and my jacket should be removed. But if I asked this question in the context I've just described, it would be idiotic because I would be missing the more obvious situation at hand. Who cares about whether or not my jacket should be removed? The house is burning down around us! In other words, there's a bigger picture happening here, so clearly the question of whether or not I should take off my jacket is not the most important or pressing issue.

Similarly, asking about God's will for your life is probably asking the wrong question. There's an assumption within the question itself that we want God to bless us with what will make us most happy because it's all about us. The question is asked through American cultural values that place control, comfort, prosperity, individualism, and safety above all else. Truthfully, the more appropriate question should be, *How does my life fit into God's will?* This is how to ask the question correctly because it's taking into account the bigger picture of how God is working in the world. It assumes the plot of the story isn't about you, but about him. He is the main character. He is doing something amazing in the hearts of people, and we should want to know how we can be a part of what is already happening as he is moving.

Do you see the difference? When we ask the question from a God-centered perspective, the entire narrative of our lives shift toward his will and good rule and away from our personal agenda. And when we rest in his kind control, our fears are quieted. When we see the larger story happening and open our eyes to the fact that we are not the hero of the story, confusion and frustration no longer hang over our heads.

As I've explained this paradigm shift to many people, the inevitable follow-up question is, *Okay, if it's about how my life fits into God's will, what is God's will?* My answer is to simply encourage the person I'm talking with to read the Scriptures. Loads of passages in the Bible directly talk about or strongly imply what the will of God is, and all we need to do is pay attention when we read. From Genesis to Revelation, we see the unfolding of God's will throughout history, because in his Word, he reveals what's on his heart, what he wants to accomplish, and what he values. If we have steady input from the Bible, we are able to see and understand how our lives can become a part of what God's plans are for humanity, thus bringing peace to our restless hearts.

When I was at the end of my junior year in college, I could see the close of my time at the university on the horizon, so I asked the Lord to lead me to some specific places in Scripture to help alleviate the pressure I was experiencing about what I should do after I graduated. I had a few options, but I wasn't sure about what to do, and that caused a significant amount of worry in my heart. I prayed, and God used a piece of the gospel of Matthew in my life to clearly lead me toward staff with Cru, the parachurch organization I still work for today.

"Then he said to his disciples, 'The harvest is plentiful, but the laborers are few; therefore pray earnestly to the Lord of the harvest to send out laborers into his harvest'" (Matthew 9:37–38).

Being in college, I knew thousands of my peers were lining up to apply for the high-paying jobs that would advance their careers and help them achieve the American dream. Few, however, were lining up to work in God's harvest field as a full-time missionary. And even though I knew missionary work wasn't "higher" or "better" than working for the Lord in a secular field, that truth from Matthew 9 struck me in a way that's guided my life ever since. When I made the decision to go on staff with Cru, I wasn't anxious anymore because I was confident in the Lord's will for my life at that time. I wasn't afraid I might be doing the wrong thing because my decision was totally in line with what the Bible communicated.

And as liberating as that confidence in God was, the actual beauty of my decision was coming to the realization that if God's will were distinctly different from what I believed he was leading me toward, he would eventually help me arrive where he wanted me to go. My job was to keep my nose in Scripture and remain sensitive to his Holy Spirit.

Subjective Means

A good friend and mentor, Roger Hershey (Hersh), travels around the globe and teaches college students how to make biblical decisions in light of figuring out their futures. Whenever he speaks on this topic, he goes through a few subjective means of helping to determine God's will when it comes to decision-making. If you feel as though you haven't really sensed anything from God after both reading through Scripture and heartfelt prayer, he offers suggestions on how to ask a few questions as you prayerfully weigh the options at hand. Hersh always says these subjective means questions are helpful, but not authoritative, when deciding what to do. They've been extremely helpful for me too, so I thought they'd be appropriate to share in light of our potentially fearful response to "not hearing from God" when we make decisions.

Here's the first question to consider: *Do I feel as if I have peace about something?* I've certainly told people on numerous occasions that I had peace about the choices I made in my life. If there was angst in my soul or negative emotions regarding a decision, it was certainly legitimate for me to say I didn't have peace about something. My sanctified mind, will, and emotions consistently influence my thinking . . . and rightly so. However, I know all too well that my emotions can also go haywire from time to time. The real question to be asking is, *Do I have peace about something because it's just the most convenient/comfortable, or is the peace I have God's peace?* It's very important to discern the difference between the two. The Bible is always the source we should rely on in relation to the search for peace. In other words, if it conflicts with Scripture, it shouldn't matter how I feel because it's wrong. As Christians, our governing authority is and always will be the Word of God, and we should always filter our lives through its Holy Spirit-inspired words. If we don't, the "peace" we think we have will become our authoritative means of decision-making, and that's certainly unsteady ground upon which to stand.

If I'm choosing something that clearly goes against what the Bible commands, it is not the correct impression, plain and simple. It shouldn't matter what my emotions or urges tell me to do—if they are in direct violation of biblical direction, they are wrong. I know testing our impressions of peace against the Word of God should seem pretty simple, but as many of us know, people constantly make excuses for why "what they feel" should be more important than the clear directive of Scripture.

From where I stand, this is the number one reason our modern society is in such confusion about truth. Culture places personal feelings at the highest level of importance when discerning the choices of life, and when our feelings trump all else, the bedrock of our decision-making will always be shaky. Feelings are fickle. They go up and down all the time. Should the compass I put my faith in be a variable with as much instability as the human emotional roller coaster? No. Emotions are important, of course, but they should not be the factor I base my life on, regardless of how much importance our culture places on them.

We also need to test our feelings of peace (or anxiety) against the wise counsel of other believers. I cannot overstress this point. During my years in ministry, I have known so many men and women who have tried to go after a number of different things: career choices, dating partners, social options, et cetera, ignoring the godly counsel of others around them, only to have their choices lead to destruction time and time again.

A close friend of mine named Rob dropped a bomb on me and a few others in our collective friend group when he told us one evening he was thinking about getting a divorce from his wife after only two years of marriage. This news was especially jarring for me as I was one of his groomsmen when he got married. My other friends and I advised him not to head down that road but instead to try and work it out with his wife. Sadly, our words fell on deaf ears, and he filed for divorce a few months later. He spent the better part of fifteen years running away from God in a lifestyle of what I like to call "party dude-hood." For many years, nearly every picture I saw of Rob online was characterized by self-ish ambition, drinking, and recklessness. He wasted so much time running away from God and ignoring the godly wisdom of his friends that he no longer had any kind of recognizable relation-ship with Christ. When we were younger, Rob was a guy I co-led a Bible study with, someone I went on mission trips with, and a person I looked up to spiritually.

Dangerous things can happen when we don't surround our-selves with men and women who walk with Jesus and are "annoy-ing enough" to tell us when they see us on a wrong path in life. Our blind spots are, by nature, blind. We need someone to lov-ingly point them out to us. Sure, we might hate what they have to say in the moment they call us out, but as we pursue godliness, we will thank them later for helping keep us on the straight and narrow. Feelings of peace about a decision are great, but test them against (a) Scripture and (b) the wise counsel of godly input.

The other subjective means question to help determine God's will in decision-making is this: *Am I relying on an open door/ closed door means of grace?* Roger Hershey certainly calls this means of understanding God's will legitimate, and even gives the biblical example of Acts 16 when the spirit of Jesus forbade Paul from going in a certain direction and God directed Paul to instead plant the first church in Philippi. Sure, when God closes and opens "doors" for us, we should pay attention, but when we rely on those means completely as authoritative, it can be problematic.

For example, there might be multiple open doors to pursue in a certain situation, so how do I know which one to go through? Or maybe, more importantly, how do I know that a certain "closed door" might not be an opportunity for God to show up and bring glory to his name in an incredible way? Moses standing in front of the Red Sea looked like a pretty big closed door. Lazarus dying was a fairly definitive closed door. Joseph sitting in a prison cell after his brothers sold him into slavery no doubt felt like a huge closed door. And Christ on the cross as "defeated" probably looked like a gigantic closed door to the disciples. But what were all of these in reality? They were opportunities for God to bring glory to himself in ways nobody could have ever imagined.

Subjective means of determining God's will for our lives are helpful, but they should not be authoritative. When we are mentally and emotionally pressed to try and figure out the Lord's will for our lives, it can be extremely stressful, and stress can lead us to unsteady ground if we aren't careful and intentional about how we step forward in life.

But as each of us mentally Google the question, *What does God want me to do?*, let's not forget we are a part of his bigger story. And in light of that grace-filled fact, we need to view ourselves in the proper perspective. He is God and we are not. It is his story, not ours.

Decision Time

Making choices can create significant pressure for many of us, especially when we are highly aware of the countless options to choose from in the various streams of life. Technology has seen to it that we are hyper aware of the millions of decisions available to us, because technology thrives on the ability for people to have options. The freedom to choose and customize our lives is great when it comes to selling smartphones, but it can be a significant catalyst for stress and anxiety when someone has trouble wading through the ocean of choices technology throws at us.

I know in the past I've asked God to simply "ping me" in some mystical way and let me know what I'm supposed to do to avoid the inevitable pressure that comes with important decision-making. But it's not about God pinging me with some supernatural clairvoyance so I can coast through life without burdens. Your time on this earth was never about sitting around and waiting for God to ping you and tell you what to do. We must not give in to the sinful desire to be passive, because passivity requires no faith. When we are intentional, however, we move out in faith and trust God will lead us as we use the mind he has given us to make decisions with initiative. Faith is not waiting around until you're 100 percent sure of what you're supposed to do; there's no faith in that. When we trust him and believe he will lead us, there's risk involved, but living in faith is always the sweet spot of life for a Christian.[1]

You might ask, "But what if I fail or make the wrong decision? What then?" Well, just as we take steps of faith and trust God will lead, we must also have faith he is big enough to cover for our mistakes, should we make them. Remember when Peter cut off the ear of Malchus, the high priest's servant who was coming to arrest Jesus in the garden of Gethsemane? What happened when Peter pulled out his sword and made that mistake? Jesus reached out, touched the servant's ear, and healed him (Luke 22:51). So yeah, I think God can cover quite well for your mistakes. I've lopped off a lot of ears in my days of ministry (metaphorically, of course). I've screwed up a ton, but Jesus can correct and use us even in the midst of poor decision-making.[2]

Look at Jonah—this prophet wasn't even following the Lord's will and God still used him. In the midst of Jonah's rebellion by going to Tarshish instead of Nineveh, God used Jonah to lead a group of pagan sailors to himself, and then he swallowed Jonah up and spit him back out in the right direction. He can do the same with you.

Your job is to take steps of faith and start to move, even in the midst of stress or confusion. Your confidence isn't necessarily in yourself and what you're capable of doing but in a good God who loves you and wants you to flourish where he leads you to go and grow.

What Does God Want Me to Do?—Reflection Questions

1. In what ways have you assumed the plot of your life story is about you rather than God? List a few examples.

2. Who is the person in your life "annoying enough" to tell you when they see you on the wrong path? If you don't know someone like that, who would be the top three people you might want to ask to be that person for you?

3. What is the one decision you're struggling with right now that's leading you to question your ability to make a decision and move forward? What steps of faith can you take to start that momentum in a godly direction?

4

What Does God Want from Me?

One of the major ways I've been able to learn more about myself is via the life-altering event commonly referred to as "becoming a parent." When my first daughter, Quinn, was born, my wife and I launched ourselves headfirst into a bunch of trustworthy parenting books because we knew everything in our lives was now different. There's a lot of great advice out there about how to rear a child, and in my frank opinion, a ton of worthless advice to go along with it . . . sometimes even in the same book.

But after poring over recommended sleep patterns, thoughts on cloth diapers, and instructional eating habits for kids, we found a piece of advice in one book that proved extremely helpful when it came to dealing with our daughter's natural disobedience and behavioral issues.

See, as a parent, you learn very quickly that children are sinners, just like everybody else on the planet. And if you don't believe me, the next time you pass by a park or playground on your afternoon walk, take a second to observe how a child reacts when another kid takes his toy. I guarantee that child's response will not be the kind of reaction that makes you feel warm and fuzzy about the innate goodness of humanity.

I knew my wife and I needed to be intentional with instructing Quinn on how to course-correct when she didn't want to obey. This piece of advice in one of our parenting books said we should teach our child to obey all the way, right away, and with a happy heart.[1]

We worked on that specific principle in our home with her, and subsequently with our second daughter, Hayden, as a norm for the Abbott household, and we've found it to be immensely helpful. In fact, I still find myself reminding the girls to obey all the way, right away, and with a happy heart when I sense rebellion brewing in their hearts.

As I have recited these words over the last years with my daughters, the Holy Spirit has chipped away at my own stubborn heart and taught me that perhaps I should implement this motto into my own life as I wrestle with my daily rebellion in relation to God.

What exactly does this repeated phrase mean for me? I'm glad I asked.

It means the clear instruction I see in the pages of Scripture is what I need to be obedient to—all the way, right away, and with a happy heart. God wants my obedience in the specifics laid throughout the Bible. For example, in places such as the Ten Commandments in Exodus 20, or Paul's instruction for my sanctification in 1 Thessalonians 4. He gives all of his followers specific instruction in Scripture, and we are to follow it all the way, right away, and with a happy heart.

When it comes to the details, they seem pretty cut-and-dried— he specifically gives instructions, and we specifically follow those instructions. That sounds fairly simple, right? Yes, but it isn't just limited to the specifics. God wants my obedience on a broad scope too. My overall heart and posture toward the Lord should be one of yielding to his authoritative rule. We were bought with a price (1 Corinthians 6:19–20), and that means we are his children. God paid for us through Jesus Christ, so we should always respectfully obey his loving instruction.

He wants me to be obedient to him in every way possible throughout my life, both in the micro (specifics) and the macro (in general). Why? Because God wants me to trust him and trust in his perfect Word.

Here's a good example of this, communicated to us in the Old Testament:

> The *law* of the LORD is perfect,
>> reviving the soul;
> the *testimony* of the LORD is sure,
>> making wise the simple;
> the *precepts* of the LORD are right,
>> rejoicing the heart;
> the *commandment* of the LORD is pure,
>> enlightening the eyes;
> the *fear* of the LORD is clean,
>> enduring forever;
> the *rules* of the LORD are true,
>> and righteous altogether.
> More to be desired are they than gold,
>> even much fine gold;
> sweeter also than honey
>> and drippings of the honeycomb.
> Moreover, by them is your servant warned;
>> in keeping them there is great reward.
>> (Psalm 19:7–11, my emphasis added)

Do you see the amazingly positive results that come from obeying God that this psalm describes for us? When we obey him, it revives our soul, develops our wisdom, makes our heart rejoice, enlightens our eyes, and gives us great reward. But not just that—in the working out of our obedience, we are obviously communing with God in an ongoing way that implies a deep bond and intimate connection with our Maker. Jesus himself said, "If you love me, you will keep my commandments" (John 14:15), and the obvious implication is that we are motivated to obedience because of relationship. We don't obey simply for personal benefit (even though Scripture says we gain that); we obey because it makes our relationship with God more rich and wholesome. God wants our obedience because he wants us, and as we obey, we get him. Being obedient to God is a win-win.

Disobedience Is Dumb

I've been alive longer than my daughters, and as a result, I naturally know more than they do. I'm smarter than they are (for now at least), and I generally know what's best for them. When they disobey me and try to do things their own way, not only is that dumb on their part, it's relatively inefficient and ineffective. When they disobey my instruction, things are usually haphazard and unproductive. They take a ton more time to get something done, and that something almost always isn't done well at all. I want my girls to obey me not only because I want things done well and in a timely matter, but also because it's what's best for them. My wise instruction in their lives is beneficial for me *and* them.

Now, let's follow that line of reasoning and take it one step further. If I've been alive for many more decades than my children, and God himself has been alive *forever*, it stands to reason he knows more than I do, right? It also makes sense that my good, heavenly Father knows what's best for me too. His benevolent wisdom is always relevant to every part of my life because he sees everything from every possible perspective.

Just like my kids, when I think I know what will be best for me, and my choices are clearly in conflict with the instruction of Scripture, I'm acting in a way that will yield inefficient and ineffective consequences. Disobedience to God *always* yields a haphazard and unproductive life, no matter how much my feelings tell me I'm on the right path. God's instruction through Scripture should always determine my decision-making, regardless of how I feel about it.

When "following my heart" becomes the filter by which my choices are made (both generally and specifically), my lifestyle will produce sinful destruction. Why? Because my heart is sinful, not trustworthy, or good! Paul tells us in the book of Romans (quoting directly from Psalm 14:3 and Psalm 53:1–3), "As it is written: 'None is righteous, no, not one; no one understands; no one seeks for God. All have turned aside; together they have become worthless; no one does good, not even one'" (Romans 3:10–12).

Jesus takes it one step further and says our problem in life isn't something external, but something that comes from within us. Check out what he says in the Gospel of Mark about what contaminates a person: "And he said, 'What comes out of a person is what defiles him. For from within, out of the heart of man, come evil thoughts, sexual immorality, theft, murder, adultery, coveting, wickedness, deceit, sensuality, envy, slander, pride, foolishness. All these evil things come from within, and they defile a person'" (Mark 7:20–23).

The bottom line is our hearts are deceitful because our hearts do not seek after God. They are wicked, and they defile us. They are crooked, devious, and desperately sick (Jeremiah 17:9). Despite the many Disney movie songs that have taught us to follow our hearts, our hearts cannot be trusted. This is radical—and as a biblical worldview, it is massively unpopular.

God, however, is upright. God is pure. His Word is perfect, and his statutes are true and righteous altogether (Psalm 19:9). God's law is flawless, and he calls us to obey it because it is always reliable.

Our fickle hearts are not the foundation on which we should build our lives or make our decisions. Obedience to his instruction revealed to us in the Bible is what he wants for us and from us because he always knows what is best. Let's obey his Word all the way, right away, and with a happy heart.

The How-To

I'm a practical guy, so I always ask the question, "So how do I do that?" If we understand God's commandment toward obedience and want to submit to the Lord in all we do, right away, and with a happy heart, how exactly do we get that done?

Well, when someone accepts the free gift God offers to us in the sacrifice of his Son, Jesus Christ, we enter into a relationship with him, and the third person of the Trinity comes to dwell inside of us—the Holy Spirit. God the Holy Spirit is like the electricity that makes our house run properly. He gives us the power to experience victory over sin and live a life of obedience in ways that never would have been possible on our own. And because he lives inside each and every believer when they say yes to the gift of Jesus, we can tap into this power anytime we want to see success.

It all happens by faith. We access the power the Holy Spirit offers by asking him to do the work of Christ within us, and then trusting he'll do what he promised. Many followers of Jesus try to live the Christian life in their own power, and this leads to frustration, anger, and eventually defeat. Trying to "just be better" or "stop your sinful behavior" to experience success in your walk with God will lead to defeat. When you come into a relationship with God, it is by faith, and in the same way, you live the Christian life by faith. Ultimate freedom from sin and a life characterized by obedience to him comes through ongoing surrender to Jesus. This can only be done by faith.

Through *faith*.

As Christians, we trust God to work in us, and bring life to the dead areas of our lives. And even though buckling down and trying harder isn't the answer, we ourselves do in fact have a role in cultivating the Spirit's influence. God calls each of us to "fan into flame" the Spirit's power and influence by "addressing one another in psalms and hymns and spiritual songs, singing and making melody to the Lord with your heart, giving thanks always and for everything to God the Father in the name of our

Lord Jesus Christ, submitting to one another out of reverence for Christ" (Ephesians 5:19–21).

Like any living space, the heart has an ambience all its own, and what Paul describes here is an atmosphere of the heart that fosters the greatest influence of the Spirit. This is the experiential reality of the kingdom of God living and laughing in our hearts, but it's an atmosphere that must be created through faith and repentance.

Faith and repentance make room for the Holy Spirit in our lives, and in that environment, we grow to love the things the Spirit loves. It's almost like a party we have to throw each day—a faith and repentance party that acts as a means by which the grace of God flows into our lives and molds us into the image of his Son.

These are the mechanisms of spiritual transformation—praising, thanking, worshipping, singing, fellowshipping—because these are the elements of a party. And this "party" plays host to the presence of God, filling us with his Spirit, and the Spirit's filling is what transforms us.

Understanding and living this out will change your life. It changed mine. Although this is still a continual struggle, finally grasping what it meant to live a victorious and obedient Christian life was the light that broke through the darkness for me. It wasn't about trying to be better. It was about allowing the Spirit of God to work in my life right now so he could usher in triumph where there was once only defeat.

What Does God Want from Me?—Reflection Questions

1. In what areas have you had a difficult time obeying God's Word? Why have those particular areas been challenging for you?

2. In what ways have your feelings been your guide when it comes to your decision-making? In seeing that our hearts are evil and not trustworthy, how do you plan to shift your worldview from the Disney movie perspective to a biblical perspective?

3. Take some time to meditate on Psalm 19:7–11 and let its truth shape your view of God, his Word, and your decision-making from here on out. Ponder what it would be like to foster the greatest influence of the Holy Spirit to work in the atmosphere of your heart.

5

How Do I Handle the Void?

A friend of mine once wrote in an online post, "I'm saving binge-watching *The Office* for marriage."[1] Pretty good, right? Not only is this statement hilarious, it's also an interesting window into the lives of people in modern times who choose to consume media in massive quantities over a short period of time. In a way, it's simply the norm that nobody would think you were weird if you told them you spent the weekend sitting on the couch, binge-watching an entire television series from start to finish.

Streaming services allow us to indulge in escapism in a way that can be all-consuming for as long as we want. And while on the surface this might sound like a great way to relieve the everyday pressures of life, it and other forms of synthetically filling the void can actually be dangerous.

You might be wondering what I mean by, "the void." The void is that nagging sense of emptiness you feel when life isn't able to distract you anymore from the misery of a heart that is never satisfied, struggles with making wrong choices, and living in a world that is also messed up and unsatisfying. The void is that longing you feel for something more than what you're currently experiencing. It's what Augustine referred to as the God-shaped vacuum in the heart of every person that cannot be satisfied by any created thing but only by God the Creator.[2] It's our innate desire for a relationship with God that we attempt to satisfy with anything but God. We can feel so empty or sad, and we crave to replace the sadness with joy or satisfaction.

When troubles come around, our knee-jerk reaction is to constantly bring life back to a state of comfort. We've been trained from birth to sidestep anything that might make us feel displeasure, pain, or emptiness and run to any kind of respite that will soothe our unsettled hearts and attempt to fill the void. Those pseudo-shelters we run to during life's storms do bring us quick feelings of comfort or relief, so we have a tendency to regularly go back to them whenever anything happens to apply the pressure to our personal universe.

However, those seemingly helpful pseudo-shelters are just that: pseudo. They're a sham, and they cannot withstand our constant need for them. As we return to them over and over, their "healing power" rapidly weakens, so our quick fix is often to increase the dosage of the sham because we think more is always better. Examples of pseudo-shelters are easy to find in anyone's life: overeating, excessive alcohol consumption, smoking weed, sexual promiscuity, watching porn, outrageous amounts of media intake, even over exercising or a desperate, unhealthy attempt to control your environment, et cetera. Nearly anything can act as a substitute for the real solution when we come face-to-face with the void. All of us have our "golden calves" of preference when we want to purge the pain or emptiness.

In Exodus 24–32, we can see the biblical mirror held up to our faces in the similar choices made by the Israelites. God's people made a covenant with him, promising to be obedient to all the words he had spoken to them and remain faithful to his commands (Exodus 24:3–8). They sealed the covenant in blood via an animal sacrifice, and afterward, God called Moses up to the mountain to wait so he might give Moses the stone tablets, "with the law and the commandment, which I have written for their instruction" (24:12).

Moses was on the mountain with God for a little over a month, and in that short period of time, God's people completely lost their way and asked their substitute leader Aaron to make them gods to worship because they had no idea what happened to Moses. Aaron immediately collected all their gold jewelry, melted it down, and fashioned a golden calf out of it, proclaiming, "These are your gods, O Israel, who brought you up out of the land of Egypt!" (32:4).

All it took was a little over a month of ambiguity for the Israelites to go from complete obedience to physical idol worship. That's it—only forty days! They do a complete 180 on the Lord, and their leader even gives credit for their freedom from slavery to the useless golden calf he just created. It's shocking!

But when we read this story, we can easily forget that we are their carbon copy. Abandoning our first love and running to pseudo-shelters (our idols) is a part of our sinful daily routine that should fill us with the same surprise and distaste we feel for these horrid examples in Exodus 32. It often doesn't, though, because running to binge drinking or pornography when we're feeling the void doesn't "feel as bad" (or weird, for that matter) as crafting a cow made out of earrings and worshipping it.

We can be surprisingly lighthearted about our obsessions when the emptiness comes creeping. Devotion to your favorite TV show, video game, or NFL team, for example, can quickly go from a normal hobby to an active God-substitute without anyone else (including yourself) noticing. It's particularly dangerous because that progression from healthy to poisonous can be extremely subtle.

When we lean on anything that's not the Lord as the storms of life hit, it's the very definition of idol worship. Removing God from his rightful place of authority over your life and replacing him with any kind of substitute means the substitute itself has become a god to you. Tim Keller puts it this way:

Anything we look to more than we look to Christ for our sense of acceptability, joy, significance, hope, and security is by definition our god—something we adore, serve, and rely on with our whole life and heart. Idols [are things] that we turn into ultimate things to give us the significance and joy we need.[3]

Now, this might seem like pretty strong rhetoric for simply running to common worldly appeasements when we're confronted with the emptiness of life, but large problems often start with tiny compromises. Anything can quickly be made into a deity in your life if you aren't intentional about leaning into the grace of God and relying on him to satisfy you when it feels like nothing will.

Handling the void is a challenge every person faces, and where you run to when it crosses your path quickly shapes the definition of your character. Your shelter in the storm is either your God or your god (little g).

We can choose moment-by-moment to seek out the Giver of life when we feel lifeless. We can confront those hollow or lonely feelings with the truth of his Word when it says,

O God, you are my God; earnestly I seek you; my soul thirsts for you; my flesh faints for you, as in a dry and weary land where there is no water. So I have looked upon you in the sanctuary, beholding your power and glory. Because your steadfast love is better than life, my lips will praise you. So I will bless you as long as I live; in your name I will lift up my hands. My soul will be satisfied as with fat and rich food, and my mouth will praise you with joyful lips, when I remember you upon my bed, and meditate on you in the watches of the night; for you have been my help, and in the shadow of your wings I will sing for joy. My soul clings to you; your right hand upholds me. (Psalm 63:1–8)

May the grace of the Lord Jesus Christ and the power of his Holy Spirit give us the ability to consistently run to him instead of a cheap substitute. In him we live and move and have our being (Acts 17:28).

How Do I Handle the Void?—Reflection Questions

1. How and where does "the void" rear its ugly head in your life? In other words, at what times are you most likely to experience a feeling of emptiness?

2. Make a list of your most common "golden calves" that act as your personal God-substitutes.

3. Reread Psalm 63 and meditate on the ways God satisfies your soul. List some of the specifics below.

The Pressure of Relationships

Section 2 will guide you through the ever-present and always-tricky realm of relationships with other people and the obvious pressure points they can produce. We're all connected to multiple people in our lives, and while some of those connections are easier than others, you probably have a significant amount of questions concerning some of the specifics. Together we'll walk through much of what you might experience on a day-to-day basis, and my prayer is that each of your relationship connections will benefit from gaining Bible-based, godly perspective in this section.

6

The Physicality of Modern Romance

The Christian dating scene is an interesting environment as of late. What was once considered abnormal, such as an overemphasis on physicality and sexuality, or a glaring lack of defining relationships, are now commonplace on the romantic front and are not only widely accepted but frequently played out and expected. These are natural pressure points for Christians in a dating relationship, as well as those wearing the label of "unattached."

Most of the world sees dating as old-fashioned and something their parents did when they were young. Sure, you'll still find lots of young people who say they have a boyfriend or girlfriend, but the idea of going out on a traditional date isn't something college students choose to do much anymore, even if they are "dating" someone. Dates nowadays generally consist of hanging out together watching television on a couch without much communication happening. Maybe a meal is involved at some point, but not a lot of intentionality goes into the modern dating scene. And as a result, ambiguity reigns supreme while physicality fills in the communication gaps. Today, the replacement for dating on a college campus is mostly about what is called "hooking up," a purposely vague catch-all term that in and of itself is nearly impossible to define.

Some say hooking up is making out. Others say it's taking your clothes off while making out. And still others say hooking up is going all the way and actually having sex. Or it can mean none of those things, and therein lies my point. The term is ambiguous. A guy can say he hooked up with someone and therefore be in the "Hookup Club," but your definition of it might be completely different than mine. Everybody's in because nobody can nail down a clear explanation of what "hooking up" actually means.

Sadly, secular, cultural norms have a tendency to bleed over into the Christian mind-set of how things should be done, and the fallout can be easily spotted in the Christian dating landscape. Most of the input Christians get on how to approach the opposite sex is from a worldly, self-focused perspective, and that information is usually graphic, detailed, and explicit. What input they do get from the Christian community is usually too little, too late, too vague, and too sanitized to be much practical help.

As you already know, I've been in college ministry for nearly two decades, and unhealthy connections with the opposite sex is one of the main reasons I see young men and women abandon their relationship with Jesus. Consequently, I'm going to take the next two chapters to cover two different pressure points young people struggle with in relation to the subject of modern romance. The first will be the tension felt as a result of living in a culture where being sexually active with your romantic partner is accepted without question as normal.

Life Inside the Fish Tank

First let me say sex is not a bad thing. Sex is a good thing . . . a very good thing. Our bodies are good things. They are God's design. He invented them, and he also invented sex. It's just extraordinarily sad we have to learn about it from the world.

Most people on the planet are interested in sex once they hit a certain age, and what they are learning over and over again from the wrong source is, "The more you practice, the better you get." Because media is fiber-optically streamed directly into our pockets via on-screen entertainment available on smartphones, people are educating themselves about sex under the tutelage of cinematographers, studio executives, cameramen, paid actors, and even pornographers.

In his book *TheoMedia: The Media of God and the Digital Age,* Andrew Byers says, "For Christians anticipating (or trying to enjoy) marital sex for the long haul, considerable unlearning is required."[1] Why? Because we are all being spoon-fed a considerable and consistent string of lies that deceive us into believing false things about sex. Things like: watching porn and having sex are inconsequential; sex is an end goal, not a beginning of something; if you're serious about the person you're with, you should be having sex; there's something seriously wrong with you if you're not sexually active, et cetera.

Yes, sex is a great thing, but it must happen within the proper context in order for it to be experienced in the most exciting, pleasurable, and godly way possible. This reminds me of a former roommate of mine and his pet fish.

Back when I was a single guy, one of my roommates had a medium-sized, twenty-gallon fish tank with three or four fish in it, positioned in his room right next to his desk. And every now and then, I would go into his bedroom to sit in his desk chair and swivel it toward the fish tank to watch the little creatures swim around their home. I did this a lot to relax a bit after a long day of work, because watching fish swim can be very therapeutic (that's why you find fish tanks in doctors' offices).

One day I found myself sitting in my roommate's chair, staring at one bright orange fish as he swam from side to side in the tank. As I watched him swim, a thought came to my brain that made me pause.

"Why should my roommate's fish be confined to this cramped little tank? It's not very big in there, and he has to share it with two or three other fish for every second of his life. That's not fair! This adorable goldfish should be allowed to experience the freedom of roaming around our entire apartment as much as he wants, without the inhibition of confinement to this measly twenty-gallon fish tank."

As these thoughts went through my head, I immediately decided what I must do to give my roommate's fish his freedom. I grabbed the little green net-on-a-metal-stick that my roommate kept on the stand next to the fish tank, I dipped the net into the water, scooped the bright orange fish up with the net, pulled him out of the watery prison he lived in, flipped the net upside down over the middle of the floor, and shouted, "You're free! Roam unhindered anywhere you'd like because you are no longer a slave to your fish tank!"

When the little orange goldfish plopped onto the carpet next to a pair of unwashed socks on my roommate's floor, I watched him wiggle around for a few moments as he opened and closed his mouth. The fish just flopped on the ground in that same spot until it stopped moving many moments later . . . and died.

Now, before you decide you hate me because of goldfish cruelty, let me tell you that this little event never actually happened. Sorry to mislead you.

Yes, from time to time I did go sit in my roommate's chair and watch his fish swim, but never did I stupidly murder one of his cute little friends. So calm down. I told you this story because of what it has the power to illustrate.

True freedom, vibrancy, and life were found for that little goldfish within the context of the water in that fish tank, and anything outside of that environment brought suffocation and eventually death. In my fictional story, even though I "freed" the small orange fish from the "prison" of his habitat where he experienced life, into the bigger, more exciting space of our apartment, the truth was what looked like liberation was in fact assassination.

And in a similar way, the world is urging each of us to experience the same kind of sexual "liberation" outside the "prison" or constraint of marriage.

"It's not fair!" says culture. "You should be allowed the freedom to sexually roam around as you please, without being confined to the boring cage of marriage! Out here is where real life can be found!" But if anything in the sexual arena is taken outside the God-given commitment of marriage, it only leads to destruction and brokenness.

See, sex exclusively within a marriage relationship isn't a prison; it's freedom. Sex within marriage is life! It is the gracious, God-created plan for the maximum experience two people can have, because they know they aren't going anywhere. They know within their marriage, there isn't any embarrassment or comparison or insecurity. They know the other person isn't going to grab her clothes and leave in the morning. There is no walk of shame for married couples, because they've committed their lives to one another in every way, not just sexually. Sex in marriage is where life is found, and sex outside of marriage, though it may look like liberation, is in fact assassination.

Sticky Notes and Envelopes

As Christians, we have three enemies—the world, our sinful nature, and Satan. And all our enemies do is lie. The Bible even goes so far as to say the devil is the "father of lies," and when he lies he is "speaking his native language" (John 8:44 NIV). There is no truth at all in anything our three enemies tell us about how to achieve a healthy sexual relationship, but the astounding thing is that nearly everyone on the planet has bought into those lies.

The Enemy would have you believe that getting married as a virgin is ridiculous because why would you "buy a car without test-driving it first?" Why on earth would you walk into marriage without knowing what your partner is like in bed? You don't really even know who he is if you've never had sex with him, right?

"You need to have plenty of sexual experiences," says the world, the sinful nature, and the devil. "Then and only then will you have a thriving, intimate relationship with your partner, because practice makes perfect."

No doubt you've heard this perspective, witnessed it in someone close to you, or even bought into it yourself. But when a bond is made via a sexual experience, it is not something that can be easily removed. Engaging in a sexual act with another person is meant to exist within a committed marriage relationship, and without that proper context, lives can quickly be destroyed.

The world's perspective would have you believe sex is just a thing that happens between two people for the purpose of experiencing selfish pleasure. Even the phrase, "get some" is intrinsically self-serving. This perspective kind of treats the act of sex like the random placement of a sticky note to any person you want to "get some" from. Stick to someone here, then peel away. If you like that person, stick to her for a bit, then peel away. Stick to the hot person you met at the bar, then peel away in the morning. Stick to the person you've had a crush on, then peel away. "Be a sticky note!"

But the catch is, sex was never created to be a temporary thing. It's a God-designed bond between a man and woman in a loving, committed marriage that's intended to build a stronger relationship over time. Sex is not like a sticky note. It's more like an envelope. I know I'm talking a lot about stationery here, but stay with me.

When a sexual attachment is made between two people, it's like an envelope flap being sealed at the opening for the purpose of creating a secure bond. And we all know what happens when an envelope is opened, right? There is permanent damage done when the ripping apart starts. Have you ever tried to use an envelope again after it's been sealed and then opened? It's kind of pointless to try, isn't it? Why? Because it was meant to be attached only one time.

The sinful perspective would have you believe sex should be treated as if everyone in the world is a sticky note. But a sexual relationship is more like an envelope, meant to be attached only once, without being pulled apart and causing significant damage. This is God's will for us and for sex: "It is God's will that you should be sanctified: that you should avoid sexual immorality; that each of you should learn to control your own body in a way that is holy and honorable, not in passionate lust like the pagans, who do not know God. . . . For God did not call us to be impure, but to live a holy life. Therefore, anyone who rejects this instruction does not reject a human being but God, the very God who gives you his Holy Spirit" (1 Thessalonians 4:3–5, 7–8 NIV).

God is brilliant. He has intentionally designed our physical relationships to give us the maximum sexual experience possible, so the less you do now, the more you end up investing into your future. Yes, godly sexual investing takes an extreme amount of patience, but patience pays off.

A Past That Brings Shame

Whenever I end up talking about the subject of sexual purity and the importance of remaining sexually pure in a romantic relationship, I inevitably end up getting asked a series of very legitimate follow-up questions about sexual impurity in the past. Shame can flood people's hearts when they hear all I've shared thus far, and questions like this rise to the surface: "Well, that's great for people who haven't messed up yet, but what about me?"

Questions like this are valid. If we neglect these kinds of issues and pretend nobody has ever messed up in the past, we are being naive and ignoring a large section of the population who longs for answers and the kind of grace that is lavishly poured out on each of us in the truth of the gospel.

Perhaps you have come to know Christ just recently, and you have a sexual history with every person you've ever dated. Or maybe you've been a Christian for quite some time, but you were still looking for acceptance and love from a boyfriend or girl-friend in your past, and that led you to some sexual encounters for which you are now ashamed. Or, perhaps, this whole concept of sexual purity is brand-new to you, and the idea of not being sexually intimate with your boyfriend or girlfriend is completely foreign because that's the way you've always been; no one has ever told you anything different. There could be countless reasons for anyone to say, "Well, all that stuff about staying pure is good, and I want to do that from this day forward, but I'll never be able to change my imperfect past."

So, what about *those* people? Honestly, I'd imagine many of you who are reading this are one of "those people," so first let me say something I hope will stick with you regardless of what your past may hold: Jesus offers healing.

If we are in Christ, the Bible says we are a new creation (2 Cor-inthians 5:17). Things that used to be true of us in our history are dead, and we are made new and perfect because of Jesus's redeem-ing work on the cross. In Christ alone is forgiveness, restoration, newness of life, and healing of our past failures. Even if you messed up after you became a Christian, you are still wholly accepted and made new by the sacrificial blood offering Jesus made for you when he hung from the tree. You can take comfort and rest in the fact that when God sees you, he does not see your past sexual compro-mises, but your newness in his Son and the blood that covers your life for all eternity. You are clean in his eyes!

And when it comes down to it, because it is only God's opin-ion that truly counts, we can move forward in our lives with confi-dence that the shortcomings of our past in the sexual area do not define us. If we are in Christ, we are all spiritual virgins, and the truth of our purity is again a testament to the goodness of God and how glorious he is.

See, it's not about how great we are or how great we can be from here on out. It's about how amazing he is because of his grace, love, sacrifice, and perfection. If you are a virgin and have never compromised in that area before, praise God for his graciousness in your life! If you have stumbled and crossed the line sexually many times in your past, praise God that he has forgiven you and offers his gracious healing in your life! Either way, God is good and gets the glory.

It's all about him.

If you have a past you are not proud of, rejoice in the fact that God has restored you to the new creation you now are. This is your identity, so rest in it and don't believe the lie that you won't be able to climb out of the pit of despair that is a sexually immoral history. Christ's sacrificial blood that buys your forgiveness is bigger than your sordid past.

Additionally, I'm not naive enough to believe that once someone becomes a follower of Jesus, they automatically stop struggling with sexual sin. I know that when the mistakes of the past become habitual, they can easily become mistakes of the present. True as that may be in your life, take heart that you still have Christ to go to for forgiveness and help in the present. When we fail today, we can move toward Christ in repentance and faith today, and in so doing, we are washed clean time and time again without even a hint of condemnation (1 John 1:9; Romans 8:1).

The Benefits

Obedience to God is ultimately a response of love, trust, and submission to his authority. Not only that, we experience the blessings of God when we live obediently to his commands laid out in Scripture. When we move forward in obedient submission to the Lord in this area, we can easily start to see how it's the ultimate way to live, despite what the world around us is shouting. I mentioned this in an earlier chapter, but I think it's important to remind ourselves of the specific benefits of obedience when it comes to romance and the temptation of physically going too far.

I'm not going to brag here and tell you I'm awesome because I waited until marriage to have sex, but what I will do is unapologetically explain to you that I'm glad I made the decisions I did. I got married when I was twenty-nine years old, and I was a virgin when I did so. So was my wife, and I have to tell you there has *never* been a time in my marriage when I've thought to myself, *I really wish I had done more sexually before I got married*. And I have certainly never thought, *I wish my wife had more experience in the bedroom before she married me.*

I praise God all the time that neither my wife nor I had sexual experiences before we were committed to each other in holy matrimony. And as a result of our choices to stay sexually pure, I've never compared her to anyone from my past, she's never wondered if she was better or worse than one of my old girlfriends, we have never worried about sexually transmitted diseases of any kind, and I've never had a flashback from a previous sexual experience when I'm with my wife. It's beautiful, and I continually give thanks to my Maker that he spared each of us in this way.

Jesus be glorified. Isn't he great? I love that God called me to a life of celibacy until I married my wife. I wouldn't have it any other way, and I can say with absolute certainty that I'm so glad we both waited because she was worth it . . . and I like to think I was too.

That said, if my story doesn't sound at all like yours and you do have a history of sexual activity, there is great benefit in living obediently to the Lord in this area from this moment onward. Repenting of your previous lifestyle and living in radical obedience to God reaps a beautiful harvest of blessing, regardless of your past missteps. Course-correcting in this realm will still lay a foundation of trust in your future marriage because intentional obedient choices speak volumes to your future spouse. They show that you actually believe what you say, and you're willing to live in a way that honors Jesus, despite what you may have done in the past.

Not only that, your testimony to the surrounding world will stand as a beacon of light that shines on Christ and communicates to a sexually rampant culture that his lordship is more valuable than your personal, sinful desires. He is worth it, and your story will shout the gospel message loud and clear. Praise be to God that you have the opportunity to be a living, breathing example of 2 Corinthians 5:17:

> Therefore, if anyone is in Christ, he is a new creation. The old has passed away; behold, the new has come.

The Physicality of Modern Romance
Reflection Questions

1. If involvement in the hookup culture has been your norm in the past, how has it left you empty, dissatisfied, or ashamed of your behavior? How does the gospel specifically address your shame?

2. How has impatience in your life led to physically compromising within the sexual arena? What kind of perspective shift can you make in your heart that will lead to making better choices in the future?

3. Reread 2 Corinthians 5:17. How should the truth of your "newness in Christ" determine your perspective about past sexual compromises? What is the truth about you, now that you are in Christ, and what kinds of choices can you make from here on out that will reap good marriage benefits in the future?

7

The Ambiguity of Modern Romance

The second pressure point I want to address in relation to modern-day romantic relationships is ambiguity, or the uncertainty of meaning in a relationship that can significantly monopolize a person's thoughts and emotions in a negative way. As I noted in the last chapter, a lack of communication between people has become relatively commonplace with college-aged adults, and as a result, people's hearts are being trampled. Jesus calls each of us as Christians to love our neighbor as ourselves (Mark 12:31), so when we don't care enough about another person to appropriately create clarity in our relationships (romantic or otherwise), we are living in disobedience to our Savior.

I recently read an article about the eighteen ugly truths concerning modern dating that young people have to deal with, and to say the very least, the piece made me sad. A few things, however, popped out in the article that gave me pause and made me wonder about the veracity of these supposed "truths."

Near the top of the list was the statement, "Set plans are dead. If you aren't the top priority, your invitation to spend time [together] will be given a 'maybe' or 'I'll let you know,' and the deciding factor(s) will be if that person has offers more fun/interesting than you on the table."[1]

While it may be true that "set plans are dead" is the norm to some, a mind-set like this shows a glaring lack of respect for the other person in the relationship. If set plans are dead, it's because the people who allowed them to die are lazy or selfish. An apathetic approach to communication is an infectious disease in modern dating. If men and women cared enough to intentionally communicate with one another—sticking to what they promised—it would easily cure this disease. Sure, there might be other things that come up when you have a date planned, but being an adult means following through with what you've committed to do with another person regardless of other "shiny" events that might compete for your attention. I believe if someone isn't mature enough to approach a relationship with respect and intentionality, he or she shouldn't be pursuing a dating relationship at all.

James 5:12 says, "But let your 'yes' be yes and your 'no' be no, so that you may not fall under condemnation." As followers of Jesus Christ, we are called to live life differently than the world around us, not getting wrapped up in the overwhelming cultural trends. Something as simple as clear communication with one another can be a breath of fresh air in our environment's stagnant atmosphere of vagueness. Be intentional about communicating well with your romantic interest, and if you say you're going to do something, follow through with your commitment. This is an honorable character quality in a man or woman that I deeply respect, and no doubt you do too.

When a person is dependable, letting her "yes" be yes and her "no" be no, she stands out from the crowd in a way that brings glory to Christ and draws others in, giving her the opportunity not only to care well for the opposite sex but to magnify the gospel so the non-believing masses can see him clearly. This is Mark 12:31 in action.

I've Got the Power

The sad article I mentioned earlier also said, "The person who cares less has all the power. Nobody wants to be the one who's more interested." This is not only sad, it's childish.

I understand the tempting appeal this kind of perspective holds when it comes to manipulation and an attempt to have power over another person in the context of a relationship because of fear or vulnerability. But isn't the reason people are sick of the dating scene (as it exists) a strong argument for rejecting fear, abandoning immaturity, and moving on to something more vulnerable, fulfilling, and godly? Dating should never be about who has more power in a relationship or caring less to feel better about the amount of control you hold over the person you're interested in. It should be the exact opposite. And the reason for that is because one of two things is going to happen in any and every relationship: you're either going to break up, or you're going to get married.

This reality should drive you not in the direction of control or power, but toward the godly way you go about the beginning and middle stages of your interaction with that person. You simply cannot build a foundation of flakiness, manipulation, or ambiguity in any relationship and expect it to flourish in a healthy way. Wrestling for this illusion of "control" because it makes you feel powerful will do nothing but harm.

No woman out there hopes to marry a man who doesn't put any effort into showing her thoughtfulness and care on a date.

"Oh, it was so precious! He texted me and said, 'Wanna hang out sometime?' And after blowing me off for three weeks, we finally got together, watched some stupid movie on his couch, and then he tried to kiss me before we even talked about anything of depth! It was almost like he didn't care about me at all! Magical!" Nope. No woman is praying for that kind of guy.

First Corinthians 13:11 says, "When I was a child, I spoke like a child, I thought like a child, I reasoned like a child. When I became a man, I gave up childish ways." God calls us to far more than the cultural status quo of relationship obscurity and childish attempts to control/manipulate hearts. Instead of moving backward into immaturity, progress forward into maturity, godliness, and health.

The gospel is about sacrifice so others may benefit. It is a steadfast concentration on the specifics of how Jesus Christ put others before himself so those others (you and I) can reap the rewards. Apathetic communication and jockeying for power in a relationship kick against the very essence of the gospel because they are the opposite of sacrifice. They have a "me first" mentality that dishonors the Christian faith and undermines the message of the gospel.

However, contentment and security in the reality of Christ's sacrifice on our behalf is the antidote to these poisonous cultural norms. When we gaze deeply into the beauty of the gospel, there is an irresistible desire in the heart of the believer to reflect Jesus's generosity and serve others. As this happens in the romantic realm, the power of the gospel draws us closer to God and closer to one another. It's a win-win.

The Digital Shield

Because of ways people communicate today via social media and texting, anyone and everyone now has a digital layer of protection around themselves, and they don't have to commit to anything. Texting is essentially talking *at* people instead of talking *with* people. When your communication relies solely on the basis of texting, you really feel no sense of accountability or responsibility to anyone, giving you the freedom to walk all over people or ignore them completely. Ambiguity strikes again. In a sense, texting has flattened and dumbed down modern romance in significant ways.

When you get to the guts of it, however, the problem isn't necessarily technology; the problem is what technology has forced to the surface in our lives: fear, laziness, apathy, and a desire for control. Naturally, these kinds of sin struggles are already present, perhaps especially when it comes to interacting with the opposite sex. So when the variable of the "digital shield" is added to the mix, the relationship or communication might seem to be better at first, but when all is said and done, they are actually worse. Let me explain.

It's scary for a guy to look a girl in the eye and ask her to go out on a date when feelings, nerves, and a sensitive heart are on the line. Frankly, it's just easier to open a dating app and swipe right to *like* someone or swipe left to *pass* and avoid all that in-person stuff. Also, I'm sure it's frighteningly awkward for a girl to tell a guy she has no desire to be more than friends when he shows obvious interest in a romantic relationship. For both sides of the equation, face-to-face relational tension can be almost unbearable, so if something like an app or a text message can be utilized from the safety and comfort of life behind a smartphone, more often than not, the involved parties will opt for it. Then any problems regarding feelings, nerves, or a sensitive heart are solved, right? The sweaty social awkwardness goes away with the mystery that ambiguity can provide, so it's got to be a good thing. Well, not exactly.

Communication through the digital shield, while "solving" the initial fear and awkwardness problem, actually creates an entirely new set of problems far greater than the first. Why? Because a precedent has been set that important communication between this particular guy and girl is going to be dealt with in the easiest way possible—a way that brings the least amount of anxiety now but, in effect, glosses over the realities of life. A couple shouldn't be in the habit of retreating to the safety of their phones or computers in times when it's hard to handle the "bumps" of relationship friction.

Albus Dumbledore once said to Harry Potter, "Dark and difficult times lie ahead. Soon we must all choose between what is right . . . and what is easy."[2]

Yes, that quote might seem silly in the context of modern dating, but what Dumbledore has to say is quite true. It's easy to shield yourself from the danger of heartache in a relationship by communicating through technology instead of face-to-face, but that doesn't mean it's right. It's important for us to push through the uncomfortable social construct and respect one another enough to spend the time and effort it takes to engage with another person in the flesh, look that person in the eye, and talk about the important things.

Handling personal things over a text message, an app, a social media conversation, or even an email when it can be done face-to-face implies retreat. It implies a lack of initiative and a selfish desire for control. This is the opposite of the call to love our neighbor as ourselves.

To the Men

Now, let me take a moment here and talk solely to the men: have face-to-face conversations with the woman you are interested in. First, if your idea of asking a girl out is typing a text message to her that says, *Hey, wanna hang out sometime this weekend?*, or worse, mindlessly swiping right on a dating app, you need to rethink your strategy. I have talked to many women who have said they wished a guy would have enough guts to talk with her face-to-face, have a plan about what he'd like to do during an encouraging evening out together, and ask her to join him.

Instead, women commonly get a series of lazy messages from guys who passively hint at the idea they'd like to hang out, saying, "Maybe you should join me," and the ladies are sick of it. Have a plan, have some guts, and talk to the girl eye-to-eye. Jesus was intentional in his pursuit of you, so follow suit and be intentional with the girl you like.

Second, if you go to pick up a girl where she lives, don't pull into the driveway or parking lot and send her a text message that says, *Here.* Park the car, get out of the car, have the courtesy to physically walk up to her door, ring the door bell, meet her roommates or parents, usher her back to your car, open her door for her, and be a gentleman. How cowardly is it of a dude when he won't even get out of the car to meet a woman's friends or family? You're not going to win any points with the people closest to the heart of your romantic interest if you hide in your car behind your phone, trust me.

Be a man and step into the social anxiety of meeting people you may not be initially comfortable with. It shows respect for her friends/family, and it communicates you care about every part of her life. When the day comes that my daughters start to date (God help me), if the boy she wants to go out with doesn't have the decency to walk to my door, shake my hand, and engage in a little chitchat with me about the weather and the latest superhero movie before he takes her out, he doesn't get to take my daughter out. It's as simple as that. (Side note: I'd also accept good conversation about football or Darth Vader.)

The girl you might like is already loved by a lot of people in her life, so take the time to meet those people and communicate that you intend to build that girl up, not remain a mystery. Love your neighbor as yourself. Mysterious boys might be appealing to some girls, but let me tell you, as a daddy, I am not impressed. I want my daughters to date boys who courageously live with integrity in the light, not boys who might use her and hide in the shadows behind the privacy of their phones.

And last, I'm not an idiot. I get the way the world works today. I know nearly all of flirting and conversation happens digitally between single people.

"Who asks a girl out face-to-face these days?" you might ask. And my answer to that question is, "Ideally, *you*." Instead of succumbing to the social norms of fearful and passive digital relational interaction, set a different kind of standard of caring for a woman by actually communicating with her personally! Not only will you stand out as a man among boys, it will also communicate care, respect, and character in a world that devalues these admirable things in men. This is the kind of guy I would trust with my daughters. This is the kind of character that magnifies gospel living.

To the Women

Women, there is tremendous danger in ascribing specific meaning to online posts when you don't know for sure what the intentions were of the one who posted. Recently I was in my car listening to a secular radio program, and the DJs were talking about the role social media played in what they called "hookups and breakups." One of the interns at the radio station had just been broken up with, so the DJs on the program were grilling her with questions about how it happened. They also wanted to know what kinds of things she did online after the breakup occurred.

The newly single girl said she immediately went to social media and stalked him. She found a message he had posted, saying he was listening to a certain album all day after their breakup. She proceeded to look up the album and go through all the lyrics to every single song, line-by-line. Eventually, she found a song with references to heartbreak. What she wanted to know was whether the other DJs thought it meant something. Was he as heartbroken as she was? Everyone on the radio program agreed it probably meant something, and the ex-boyfriend was mourning the breakup just as much as she was.

But as I listened, I thought to myself, *Uh, no, it doesn't.* They had no idea what it meant. The post that ex-boyfriend made could have meant something totally different, or even nothing at all other than the fact that he liked a particular album. But, of course, my opinion didn't matter. Everyone in the studio was certain it meant something. I'm sure the group consensus made the broken-up-with girl feel better, but the whole conversation was telling.

Women, I know about the natural fear you might have of being hurt or unloved. It can be very easy to travel down a certain mental road when you read something that's been typed by a guy; however, jumping to conclusions on relational things that are vague can create anxiety in your heart and keep you focused on the wrong things for a very long time. There is an extreme amount of ambiguity in social media. People post online all the time that could be intended in one way, but interpreted in another. Certain things, like sarcasm, for example, are easy to misunderstand.

I have known quiet and reserved people who, for whatever reason, come across as loud and even obnoxious online. Just because someone TYPES EVERYTHING IN ALL CAPS WITH SEVEN EXCLAMATION POINTS AT THE END OF EVERY SENTENCE DOESN'T MEAN THEY ARE A BOISTEROUS PERSON IN REAL LIFE!!!!!!! LOL!!

Assuming a guy means something when he doesn't state it explicitly is an incorrect assumption and could end up hurting you. Don't let the ambiguity of poor communication on the guy's part lead you to jump to conclusions. Be careful how you interpret because you are important.

You matter. God sees you. He adores you. He delights in you. And he is enough for you. You don't have to wonder what he thinks about you or throw an Instagram filter over your life in an attempt to look more attractive to him. Jesus's blood is the perfect Instagram filter that washes away all of our blemishes, and as a result of his work on the cross, we are captivating in his eyes. He accepts us just as we are—his. (Was the Instagram filter thing too much? Sorry, I felt like running with the metaphor.)

My Heart

I hope you understand my reasons for mentioning a few of these things. My heart isn't to scold you, but to help set you up for success and push you toward the gospel. We have a responsibility to live above reproach and with integrity as followers of Christ. The pitfalls can be plentiful and even alluring when it comes to today's culture. And although the temptations can be slightly different for men and women, recognizing them is the first step in avoiding the negative effects ambiguity can have in our relationships with the opposite sex.

What was true thousands of years ago is still true today—humans crave connection. Much in today's culture can drive us to make foolish decisions, especially when it has to do with the dating world. But blind acceptance of our society in the romantic sphere simply because it's "normal" doesn't necessarily instigate good or godly decision-making. Generally, it has the tendency to lead people away from rational, mature, and godly choices if our hearts aren't in check. Be sure to process your motivations before the Lord as you approach the dating scene, and make sure those motivations aren't constructed on a foundation of the path of least resistance. That isn't a bedrock you want to build your life upon.

Instead, rest contently in the message of the gospel, knowing that God was willing to die to be with you. When you embrace the magnitude of his actions on your behalf, all of your motivations and relationships will stand on the solid foundation of Christ's sacrifice.

The Ambiguity of Modern Romance
Reflection Questions

1. Read James 5:12 again. How have you failed to let your "yes" be yes and your "no" be no in dating relationships? How can you be intentional about making better choices in the ways you communicate and stick to your commitments?

2. Reread 1 Corinthians 13:11. What would it look like for you to give up childish ways in your romantic life? List a few ways.

3. How is your desire to be "normal" driving your social media persona? What intentional steps can you take right now to be countercultural and live a godly life both online and in your romantic relationships?

8

Wrestling with Parental Guidance

When you're a student, specifically a college student, it's safe to say a lot of you probably have a weird relationship with your parents in comparison to how it was back in high school. They are these people who—after being your governing authorities for eighteen years—are still giving you the ability to go grocery shopping and buy textbooks. But now they aren't really calling the shots with how you live out your daily life. You used to depend on them for nearly everything, and you (probably) naturally surrendered to their authoritative guidance, but that's just not the case now.

This is an uncommon time of "limbo" where your parents aren't in charge of you anymore, but they're still kind of in charge of you because you're not on your own in the real world just yet. And because of this unique time period, there's great possibility for tension. In other words, you're probably ready to be in control of every facet of your own life, but because you're still dependent on them, there's an existing tether to Mom and Dad's rule.

As frustrating as this limbo time can be while you're at college, let me tell you I understand how you're feeling, and I'd love for you to learn from my missteps in the past. I had a mixed bag of making some great choices in relation to my parents and some poor ones as well.

As a college student, it's important to strike a healthy balance between autonomous decision-making, and respect for your parents' wishes. It's easy when both of your desires line up and everything is harmonious, but when there's a difference of opinion, how do you appropriately wrestle with their disagreement? Of course, there are many different scenarios depending on who God has placed in your life as parents or guardians, so instead of getting too specific and thus alienating most of you, let's first talk more generally about our biblical call to submit to the ultimate authority—God himself.

Dependence and Surrender

The life God wants us to live begins with the staunch realization that we are absolutely helpless and hopeless apart from his empowerment. We desperately need God in the mental, physical, and emotional valleys, because those low points in life are often where we come to the end of ourselves, giving room for the greatest spiritual growth to occur.

God is exceptional at constantly bringing us to times when we feel out of control. He'll use health problems, financial issues, desires, habits, sin patterns, family complications, or whatever it takes to shake us free from us. And when that magical moment comes when we finally let go of our desire for control, our only option is to depend on him. In fact, he will specifically engineer circumstances so we feel out of control.

Mark 4:35–41 describes an incident when the disciples of Jesus moved from casual spectators of Christ's work in the world to actual involvement in the lesson he taught. They just heard Jesus talk about the kingdom of God via a few parables about seed, and afterward he suggested they all hop in a boat and head toward the piece of land on the other side of the water.

All of a sudden, this huge storm popped up as they were in the boat, and the waves were so crazy, the disciples began to fear for their lives. Which was saying something, because a lot of the disciples were fishermen who spent a significant amount of time around water. They could tell the difference between a regular squall and a life-threatening storm. This was the latter.

Meanwhile, Jesus was asleep on a cushion in the stern, apparently so tired from all the teaching and healing that an outrageous monsoon wouldn't even wake him up. The men were apparently disturbed enough by their predicament that they woke Jesus up and asked him if he cared about the fact that they were all going to die. He got up, rebuked the wind, and told the sea to settle down . . . and nature obeyed.

All of the men were probably standing in the boat, soaking wet from the rain and the sea, aghast by what just happened in front of their eyes, and Jesus said to them, "Why are you so afraid? Have you still no faith?" (Mark 4:40).

The disciples looked at one another and said, "Who is this guy?" But back up a second and look at verse 35, just before the twelve disciples experienced this life-threatening storm while they were on a boat with Jesus: "On that day, when evening had come, he said to them, 'Let us go across to the other side'" (Mark 4:35).

Do you see that? *Jesus* was the one who intentionally led his disciples into the storm. He was aware of what was about to happen to the disciples because he was, you know, God. Jesus made the suggestion himself, knowing full well they were about to enter a life-threatening storm. He wanted his disciples to be men of faith—men who depended on him.

Now, I don't know about you, but I am oddly comforted by revelations like this when I read them in Scripture. I love the fact that I can see and point to the evidence that God orchestrates difficult scenarios for the ones he loves. It's a part of the molding process, and I can either be afraid of it, or embrace it as a special blessing of grace he has chosen to heap upon me. I must depend on God when control dissipates.

So the first part of understanding what it means to walk by faith is dependence. The second is active surrender. Dependence and surrender are complementary toward each other, and they go hand in hand nicely when we talk about our struggles with trying to control everything. We cannot fully surrender our wills until we are convinced our situation is hopeless. As long as we're able to spot a way out, we'll probably go for it.

If you were to ask any lifeguard what the standard procedure was for rescuing a drowning person in a large body of water, he would tell you it's imperative to leave someone alone until that person comes to a point of surrender. Meaning, if a drowning man believes he can rescue himself, he will continue to kick and flail about in the water as a danger to himself, or anyone else trying to help him. To complete the rescue and not get dragged down by the drowning person, a lifeguard is trained to swim up to the point where she is just out of the reach of the man. Once he finally gives up, stops flailing, and starts to go under, that's when the lifeguard should make her move and rescue him from drowning. Until the man in the water gives up, he isn't really in a position to be helped. He must surrender to the aid of the lifeguard.

Similarly, as long as we believe we can control things, we aren't willing to surrender our lives to the God who created us. We'll work against him rather than with him in the process. But when we realize we can't make it on our own, we are like a drowning man surrendering to the hand of his rescuer. Freedom and life are not found in trying to govern every aspect of our entire lives. They are found in active dependence on the Lord and his plan, and active surrender into his care for our well-being, even when we aren't able to see it.

If you really believe in someone, you will trust that person. But if you cannot trust the person, you instinctively work to control him. Likewise, if you are wrestling with God for control of your life, it's because you don't trust him. You're afraid he doesn't know what's best for you, and you yourself would be better suited to rule authoritatively over your life.

But this is obviously not true. Your life is not a customizable series of apps on a smartphone. And while it may be hard to believe, God actually loves us more than we love ourselves. I know that's difficult for me to wrap my mind around, because I think I'm my own biggest fan, but there is One greater than I who loves me more deeply than I could ever love myself.

Don't let your desire to control your life control your life (yes, you read that right). Rest in his care and guidance, and look at verses like this with new eyes and open hands:

> Trust in the LORD with all your heart, and do not lean on your own understanding. In all your ways acknowledge him, and he will make straight your paths. (Proverbs 3:5–6)

The Fifth Commandment

It's clear we are biblically called to surrender our lives to the authority of God, and I wanted to make sure we put first things first. That being said, our parents are not God . . . you probably know this already. They are, however, the parents God has placed in our lives, and it's important to understand how we are to live out the fifth of God's Ten Commandments when it says, "Honor your father and your mother" (Exodus 20:12).

In her book *This Changes Everything*, teenage writer Jaquelle Crowe gives a helpful framework to her young readers when she talks about how to act toward their parents, thus fleshing out what it means to practically honor them. Her points are to learn from their wisdom, obey their authority, mature from their discipline, be grateful for their care, and treat them with genuine kindness.[1] She also points out the Bible gives us a compelling image of Christian parents, because they are teachers (Proverbs 1:8–9), authorities (Ephesians 6:1), disciplinarians (Proverbs 13:24), and individuals (Genesis 1:27). Our earthly honoring of them reflects our honor for the greater heavenly One.

However, not every parent follows Christ or acts in a godly way when it comes to rearing and shepherding their children, and that must be considered here. Crowe also addresses this unfortunate reality some of us face by stating,

> Obey your parents as much as you can, until you reach a point where you are asked to sin. Your obedience stops there but not before. And on the days when you wrestle with discouragement or frustration, remember you have a heavenly Father who is perfectly faithful, perfectly loving, perfectly kind, perfectly trustworthy, the perfect parent in every way. And he loves you with an unshakable love.[2]

This is well-put and immensely helpful as we consider the how-tos of living life under our parents, taking full consideration of their relationship (or lack thereof) with God. I had a student who wanted to come to a week-long evangelism conference with Cru during spring break his sophomore year, but was frustrated by the fact that his parents were adamantly against him going. His folks were not Christians, and they hated the idea of him spending his spring break talking to others about Jesus instead of coming home to work and spend time with them. This student asked me what he should do, and I told him the decision was ultimately his to make, but he needed to consider a few things as he thought about what to do.

He was still financially dependent on his parents, and they were graciously providing for his needs while he was at college, therefore he needed to respectfully honor his father and mother, and not just write them off because they weren't believers. However, I also mentioned that if he wanted to continue to follow Christ, one day he would have to draw a "line in the sand" and pursue the things

God wanted him to pursue, despite the fact that his mom and dad would disagree with him. He could draw that line now, or in the future, but eventually it was going to have to happen.

In the end, he did decide to come to the evangelism conference, but in the process, he made sure he communicated love and admiration for his parents too. He told them he respected them, but he really believed God wanted him to spend his spring break talking with others about Christ at the conference. His parents still disagreed, but they appreciated his intentional communication with them as a means of displaying his respect and care. They felt honored even though they didn't agree with him, and he was able to be obedient to God by attending the conference and sharing his faith.

Our parents are intended to be our models of the authority structure the Lord has crafted between us and him. But parents are sinful, and they make mistakes all the time. We as children sadly get a front-row seat to all of their errors, so our sin and theirs gets consistently woven into the fabric of our family dynamic. This obviously needs to be taken into consideration as they instruct us and exercise their authority over us, because it's never okay to sin even if our parents are telling us to do so. God is our ultimate authority, and we will all be held accountable to him.

When we honor our parents in a healthy, biblical way, we are in turn honoring the authority of God and bringing glory to his name. It's not always going to be perfect, and family issues are often the messiest in our lives, but when we submit control of our lives to God first, we are much more aligned to a healthy connection of reverence and respect for our parents in the midst of their sin and ours too.

Just because you're a college student doesn't mean the authoritative structure God has orchestrated between you and your parents is now severed. You may not be a child anymore, but it's the important call of God to honor your parents in deference to the Lord. In doing so, it enriches your relationship with Dad and Mom while simultaneously bringing glory to your Creator.

Wrestling with Parental Guidance
Reflection Questions

1. How does the fact that you're not a child anymore factor into your perspective of your parents and their desires for your life? Do you have trouble respecting them and their opinions? Why or why not?

2. Why is it important to be actively dependent and intentionally surrendered to God and his authority over our lives? Why is this significant to think about first as we process our parents and their role in our lives?

3. Has it been tough for you to obey the fifth commandment and honor your parents? Why or why not?

9

Is True Friendship Possible?

Growing up in a military family with the lifestyle of moving about every two years was difficult to say the least, but the experience of constantly changing my environment shaped me into the person I am today, and for that I can't complain. If I'm honest and was given the opportunity to go through it all again, however, I don't think I would choose the life of an "Air Force brat."

Why? Well, as a kid, change was a natural part of my routine, and making new friends was a large part of the adaptation process. It was important to be able to have good friends in a place that, upon arrival, was completely foreign to me. And although I understood this concept quite well, I was naturally shy and fairly inflexible when it came to pioneering new life adventures. Consequently, the common parental adage of "go make some new friends" was a rather large obstacle for me.

We all know kids can be quite cruel, and it was hard to always be wearing the "new kid" label. One particular memory that springs to the forefront of my mind happened at the beginning of my sophomore year of high school. My ninth-grade year was spent in northern Virginia, surrounded by familiarity because of the rare four-year stint my stepdad spent stationed at the Pentagon in Washington, DC. But new orders meant a new home, so before my second year of high school, we packed up and headed off to Montgomery, Alabama. When the summer ended and the fall semester started, I found myself as one of only two new kids at a small private Christian school, populated by kids from well-off families who, in their leisure time, enjoyed torturing almost anyone who showed any sign of weakness.

Cut and zoom to the metaphorical target indelibly printed on my face.

One particular day after two weeks of sitting with the other new guy during lunch, he was invited to join the popular dudes at their table, so when I arrived at our normal spot, my only friend was nowhere to be found. He literally left me by myself at the end of a long cafeteria table with nothing but my peanut butter and jelly sandwich and a looming sense of dread.

Now, ask any high schooler and he'll tell you there is no worse time to fly solo than at lunch. Social sensitivity goes up when kids eat, I guess, and consequently, being alone at the table that day left me horrified. There were no such things as cell phones back then, so I didn't even have the internet to keep me company. Even now as I recount this story, I can still vividly remember the knot in my stomach that quickly formed when I found myself all alone in the cafeteria that day. It was terrible.

I sat by myself for a solid ten minutes until, finally, one of the nicer girls in the school walked over to me and extended a merciful invitation to join her and her friends for the remainder of lunchtime. I quickly accepted her invite and breathed a small sigh of relief, knowing full well that joining her at the girls' table was in itself another body blow to my pride. Ugh, what an awful moment in my life. I wouldn't wish it on anyone.

Why am I sharing all of this with you? Well, the reason isn't to make you feel sorry for me (although you probably do), but to illustrate that without friendship and companionship, we feel lost.

In that moment during my sophomore year at the cafeteria table, all I wanted was a friend to sit with me so I could feel accepted in a new school. He went to go sit alongside another group of people, leaving me behind with a pit in my stomach and a lingering feeling of solitude.

The story doesn't end there, of course. I eventually made some new friends that year and connected with a few people who didn't ditch me during lunch. It got better, and nothing like that happened to me ever again.

But no doubt, you can probably relate to my story in one form or another. Most of us have a tale of relational isolation or abandonment that has deeply wounded our hearts. It's common to get hurt when we let people into our little worlds and trust them with our feelings. And the kind of pain we experience when a friend injures us can sting enormously because of the very fact that we *do* trust them. Experiences like this perhaps lead some people to abandon the idea of close friendships altogether. They do this because they are afraid of being hurt again. And while that is completely understandable, it is, of course, a mistake.

Unfriended

The term "friend" means something totally different today than it did when I was in grade school. For one, it can now be used as a verb because of social media, and it's also utilized online as an official label, announcing to the world one's relationship status.

However, the odd thing about the friend label is while it might come across as more authoritative online, the sad truth is that the designation today really holds no meaning whatsoever. I, for example, have thousands of friends on Facebook, yet I would only identify roughly one-third of those people as my true friends . . . even less, maybe.

Being friends with someone online has come down to a simple confirming click of a button, and the relationship really doesn't have any significance. We collect people like baseball cards and look at them more as followers than friends. Fans, even. And while this approach to friendship might feel safer and less frightening than face-to-face relationships, I would argue it's not really friendship at all.

Recently I had a conversation with a high school student named Ethan who took pride in the fact that he had more "friends" than most of the other people in his grade at school. He boasted to me about how he was able to promote music for the band he played in with incredible ease because he had a built-in database of "friends" to advertise to anytime he wanted to boost sales or song downloads. I remember thinking at the time I spoke with Ethan that he didn't really look at his friends online as true friends. They were customers—people he could exploit to get something from them.

How guarded, I thought. *And sad.*

Is that self-centered view of friendship really something we as Christians should be proud of? Or more importantly, is that attitude about friends honoring to Jesus Christ, the man who laid down his life for his friends (John 15:13)?

This Is Edited Content

If you truly want to know a person, spend quality time with her. If you only know someone within the context of cyberspace, there's a real possibility you know her far less than you think you do. If you want to know me, for example, you need to spend time with me. You can sort of get to know me if you read about me in my online profiles, but honestly, my profiles are all stuff I've carefully crafted to portray a polished image of myself. I don't ever post a picture of myself I don't like (unless I'm trying to be funny). I don't ever type something out on social media I think will make me sound stupid (again, unless I'm trying to be funny). Everything I'm putting out there is an edited version of my true self, so a strong argument could be made that online Shelby isn't really Shelby at all. It's a refined and dressed up Shelby without the flaws.

But if you were to spend any significant amount of time with me, you would quickly discover that I am extremely flawed. The online version of me doesn't always reflect my true nature because I'm actually *not* perfect, even though my public profile might argue otherwise.

And guess what? Neither are you.

If we know a person solely via the veneer of social media profiles, we don't know that person entirely. Sure, we can begin to understand who a person is by reading what he appreciates, what bands he listens to, what kind of entertainment he enjoys, and what restaurant he'd like to eat at this weekend, but that's only part of the picture. We're deceiving ourselves if we buy into the fact that we can get to know someone deeply if we only communicate via social media. Typing someone's name into a search engine might partially fulfill your curiosity about someone, but you were created for much deeper relationships than that. Being afraid of people truly knowing you shouldn't corner you into a life of digital shallowness masquerading as a multitude of friends.

The real you is the real you, and you shouldn't want your friends to only experience the polished version of your actual self. When things progress the way God created them to in the human relational experience, your friends will eventually see through the shine of your edited self. Now, that might terrify you, but relationships are meant to be that way—they're messy, complicated, and designed for emotional depth.

I recall multiple poignant moments during my younger years with some of the guys I called my best friends when we'd cut through all the goofiness and finally get real with one another. Those times were hard and kind of scary, but that's when the true bonding happened. Was it intimidating to go deeper? Of course it was! I was afraid of being rejected if I opened up and got vulnerable in our conversations. But looking back, those were some of the best times with my friends because we were willing to dig past the surface of fart jokes and our opinions about how many *Fast and Furious* movies Hollywood was going to make. Going deeper with them was extremely important, and as a result, I still call those guys some of my best friends today.

As another example, there's even a moment I remember from my dating experience with Rachael when we became truer friends and I felt the layers peel back, revealing a deeper side of the "real me" than anyone had ever seen before. It was simultaneously terrifying and wonderful. At the time, I was tempted to withdraw for fear she wouldn't like what she saw, but instead I moved further toward vulnerability with her, and our relationship only got better. She began to see a more complete picture of who I was, and it made the connection between us more authentic.

This kind of genuine friendship cannot happen to the degree you long for solely via digital media. It will always lack depth because it can never be a substitute for the real thing. A good friend and coworker of mine Keri Armentrout puts it this way: "Social media should never be a substitute for relationships, but a springboard for relationships."

I love this. When we harness the potential of social media and employ it as a springboard for something deeper, God can use it for many great things. We shouldn't let the fear of being truly known generate an excuse for multiple shallow online relationships. I'm not saying engaging with social media and connecting with people online is a bad thing, but if it's the only way we're participating in relationships, we are missing out on the joys of authentic connections with others in the way God intended it. Use social media as a launching point toward real depth, but don't allow social media to isolate you from the reality of connecting with other people face-to-face.

It Is by Design

C. S. Lewis wrote, "Friendship is unnecessary, like philosophy, like art . . . it has no survival value; rather it is one of those things that give value to survival."[1] A good paraphrase translation of that quote might be something like this: friendship—it's not food, water, or oxygen, but it makes life worth living.

Each and every person walking this planet needs to be connected in some way to another human being or beings. This is just a fact. And the piece of evidence that proves my point lies in the punishment prescribed to any individual deemed unworthy to interact with others. I'm talking about the penalty a person must pay if she acts badly when she is already in a place of punishment—solitary confinement.

We've all seen the movies or television shows that reveal to us the "worst of the worst" and take us into the jail cells of people who have been really, really bad. So much so, they can't even be allowed to spend time with any of the other criminals. They are locked away all alone by themselves. As people, we understand dishing out the sentence of "solitary confinement" is a pretty serious consequence because it strips a person of the necessary human contact each and every one of us craves. This is demonstrated well by Tom Hanks's character in the film *Cast Away*.

In the movie, Tom Hanks (spoiler alert!) plays Chuck Nolan, who is in a plane crash and marooned on a little island by himself for over four years. In the early months of being stranded, he finds a Wilson brand volleyball that he famously personifies into his only friend on the island. Nolan talks to it, argues with it, reasons with it, and even almost dies trying to rescue it at one point. Yes, a volleyball.

Now, if you haven't seen the movie, summing up that part of the film as I did in just a few sentences probably makes you laugh. However, if you've seen the movie, you know Wilson the volleyball has truly become Nolan's only friend, and losing it would be tragic. The volleyball is his only sense of connection to humanity and relationship. Without Wilson, he would have gone completely insane.

Like Chuck Nolan in *Cast Away*, you were not meant to live life alone. You and I need regular emotional, spiritual, and physical connections with people who are genuine—because that is the way God created you. That is the way the Creator designed it. That is the way the Creator designed *you* (Genesis 2:18).

We are meant for relationship, so the value we place on proactively connecting with true friends in the context of relationship is equivalent to the kind of people we will eventually become. So . . . who do you want to become?

Ralph Waldo Emerson said, "The only way to have a friend is to be one."[2] Being a good friend is a godly thing. Fear of the past shouldn't prevent you from such a beautiful, relational experience. Godly friendship sets you up for a healthy life that brings glory to Jesus and joy to your soul . . . especially when difficult times arise in your life.

When Issues Hijack

Hard times and suffering can have a tendency to overwhelm a person's heart, causing ridiculous amounts of pressure in a person's life. The importance of authentic friendships in dark and difficult times like those cannot be overstated. We truly need friendly anchor points within life to keep us not only grounded in the fundamental truth of God's Word but to help us through the times when our negative reactions to hardships consume us and we aren't thinking clearly. Friends can do an amazing job at relieving the pressure.

There's a lot of power in terror. In fact, it is such a strong motivator, it can easily dictate our every move if we aren't careful. You've probably seen a reality show or two that highlights individuals who are driven by fear so deeply they live abnormal lifestyles. The feeling of dread can push people to never exit their houses, never throw anything away, or never trust another human being. These people are possessed by terror for various reasons, and they need others to get involved in their lives so they can break free from the bondage of paralyzing fear.

I'm going to get vulnerable here for a minute and tell you I'm terrified of slasher movies. Yes, yes, I know you're *very* surprised that someone as manly as me (sarcasm implied) can be scared of something as ridiculous as teenage horror films, but it's true. In fact, against my better judgment back in college, I was challenged by a friend of mine to watch a very popular horror flick with a number of other people one evening, so I caved under the peer pressure and sat through the entire thing. Needless to say, it scared the mess out of me, and I hated the movie. The real problem came, however, in the following weeks after our little group movie night. I kept having this persistent nightmare that the serial killer from the movie was chasing after me down the hallway of our apartment. I'd run into my bedroom and slam the door, but he'd always kick it open and lunge at me with the hunting knife he used to kill his victims.

I'm not kidding, for nearly a month, I would wake up in hot sweats, terrified I was going to be killed by a fictional movie murderer in my college apartment. It got to the point where I literally had to confess my sin to the Lord that I wasn't trusting him with my life, and he needed to help me get over the irrational fear from the movie I saw. I also talked to a few of my roommates and told them about the nightmares I was having. I asked them to keep me accountable to trusting God with my well-being and that I would not live in fear. And even though they poked fun at me for being scared of the movie we all saw together, those friends helped me get over my irrational angst by pointing me toward Christ.

At the time, this issue was hijacking my life, and my friends became the conduit of God's freeing power over my irrational problem. I needed them to help me by reminding me of who God was and how I was viewing him improperly. They reminded me of his sovereignty clearly communicated in the Scriptures, and how he constantly urges his children to "fear not." It was healthy, necessary, and bonding all at the same time.

Let Me In

We are designed to be in relationship with one another, and while this might seem extremely obvious to some of you, many find it difficult to allow others into their lives and peel back the layers for another person to witness. Vulnerability is extremely hard for a wide variety of people for multiple reasons, but when you boil down those reasons, you usually end up with the same base elements—fear of being hurt, not wanting to experience rejection, a traumatic or painful past repeating itself, et cetera. Anxiety about dissonant memories and a resistance to vulnerability can be large roadblocks to authentic connection with true friendship.

There's no question, friendship is risky. I think we've all been hurt by a friend in the past, but we mustn't let the fear of getting hurt prevent us from truly wonderful bonds. That being said, forming a strong bond takes work, and work is . . . hard.

Most of the time, friendships begin in a very natural way, and they are somewhat easy to maintain if a meaningful connection exists between two people. But as most of us know, things don't always stay that way. The very wise book of Proverbs says, "A friend loves at all times" (17:17).

As we think about rejecting shallowness and moving toward thriving friendships, we will want to engage with the natural work it will take to maintain those friendships. We love because he first loved us (1 John 4:19), and as we are changed on the inside by the power of the Holy Spirit (the churchy word for that is called "sanctification"), we are given the desire by God to go deep with people in ways we never would have before we knew Christ.

When I became a believer in college, all of a sudden I had an overwhelming desire to be real with other Christians. I didn't want to hide behind a facade of "having it all together" anymore, because that was a defining characteristic of the old me. I wanted to move beyond the surface level with my friends to know them and be known by them—flaws and all. It was liberating and frightening at the same time, but I craved it because it had been spiritually hardwired into me as a new creation (2 Corinthians 5:17). Consequently, I experienced more authentic friendship with people than ever before in my life, providing depth and connection in ways I never knew were possible between friends.

Discipline and Spunk

Jesus is our perfect example of what it means to be committed to inconveniencing yourself for the benefit of others. A friend loves at all times, and the kind of work it takes to pull that off only happens through the power of the gospel. Jesus does the work for us, providing our souls with the desire to love our friends despite the fact that we know relationships can be difficult. Deep friendship can be difficult. But like anything we think is worth it, we should work fervently in the power of the Holy Spirit to build vulnerability and maintain our friendly relationships.

First, you need to be disciplined. If you want to get in shape, you need to commit to a regiment of repeated exercise. If you want to gain muscle mass, you need to methodically hit the gym and lift weights. If you want to drop a few pounds after a season of liberal munching during the holidays, you have to control your diet in the new year. All of these things take discipline. And by definition, discipline is the habitual practice of training yourself to obey a certain code of behavior to achieve a particular goal.

Discipline, of course, is not only required for getting in shape or losing weight; it's also necessary when it comes to maintaining healthy friendships. You need to take the initiative and be intentional about working on your friendship, just like anything else that's important in your life. If you neglect the friendships in your life because you're afraid to get vulnerable, they will wither and atrophy like the muscles you don't work out.

It takes discipline to intentionally communicate with someone when you're tired or busy or it's inconvenient for you, but that's what good friends do. It takes discipline to meet someone for coffee early in the morning when you've been up late the night before, but if you make the commitment, you need to follow through with it, because that's what a friend does.

Through the power of the gospel, invest in your friendships now in spite of your hesitations and you will see the fruit of that investment in the future, I promise. Friendship takes effort, and like most anything that requires discipline, the effort of working at your friendship will pay off.

A guy I knew from my early days in college ministry named Tom used to come out to our large group meeting every Thursday night and attend every social event that was thrown on the weekend. Nearly everyone knew Tom's name, but nobody really knew Tom himself. No matter how many times we invited him to come to a small group hangout, Bible study, or weekend retreat that would take things deeper, Tom would refuse. Consequently, Tom's involvement with our ministry dwindled, and after the first semester of his freshman year, I didn't see him again until a couple months before he was ready to graduate. We bumped into each other at a mutual acquaintance's house, and Tom was literally holding a huge bottle of vodka, periodically taking sips. He was completely hammered, and in his drunken stupor, he told me college had basically sucked and he couldn't wait to get out of school.

I wondered after seeing him that night if Tom would have enjoyed his college experience and flourished while at school if he had connected in a more deep and meaningful way with godly men and women who cared about him past the exterior. I didn't think, of course, our campus ministry would've been the perfect magic solution for Tom's social connection problems, but I did wonder what could have happened if he would have decided to reject the obvious fear he'd had and gone deeper to let people into his life.

Jesus changes hearts, and he gives us the ability to be vulnerable in areas we never thought we'd be able to express to another person. But because we are new creations in the power of the gospel (again, 2 Corinthians 5:17), what we once thought was impossible can now be commonplace in our friendships if we simply follow Jesus's lead and love at all times by being real with one another.

Secondly, a solid friendship needs something I like to define as "gumption." Spunk. Oomph. Moxie. Get-up-and-go. Basically, it means being a humble, compassionate voice of truth to the other person even when it's difficult to play that role.

This applies to more than just the natural obstacles that arise in a relationship because of environment, timing, or outside influence from other people. Yes, we need to be there for our friends in those situations, obviously. But the going really gets tough when we find ourselves in a situation that requires us to personally confront a friend. This can mean taking a risk and discussing something difficult because it will ultimately help and build up your friend to be more like Jesus.

A Christian friend of mine started dating a girl who wasn't a follower of Christ, and I knew immediately I needed to talk with him about it and help him make better decisions. We got together for lunch one day, and I talked with him about 2 Corinthians 6:14 that says, "Do not be unequally yoked with unbelievers. For what partnership has righteousness with lawlessness? Or what fellowship has light with darkness?"

I asked him, "If Jesus is number one in your life, why would you want to fasten or 'yoke' yourself to someone who doesn't understand this?" It was difficult, but I told him he needed to have enough patience not to settle for someone who didn't know Jesus, have a relationship with him, or claim his lordship in her life. I didn't want him to end up frustrated with her in the future if she didn't ever seem to "come around" and decide to engage in a relationship with God, and I certainly didn't want him to walk away from his faith because she had dragged him down.

He understood where I was coming from and appreciated my boldness in approaching him because he trusted me and knew I loved him. On account of our history together in the years leading up to our lunch conversation that day, my friend believed the best in my intentions because I had been there for him in times that were difficult for him and inconvenient for me. I had built a platform of trust with him, and he knew I wanted what was best for him because he knew me.

Ultimately, he broke up with the girl and was thankful he did. As a man married to a Christian woman now, my friend certainly sees the excess of bad consequences that could have come by being attached or "yoked" to someone who doesn't follow Christ.

It's been said true friends stab you in the front,[3] meaning we need to talk with our friends about any issues we may see becoming a potential stumbling block toward godly growth in their lives. This is in contrast to succumbing to the temptation toward passivity or fear or deciding to talk about your friends behind their backs. And even more appropriately for Christians, Proverbs 27:6 says, "Wounds from a friend are better than many kisses from an enemy" (NLT).

I would much rather have a friend say a hard challenge to me and raise the bar of expectation for my life than to have an enemy pat me on the back via false sentiment. And if your friends aren't willing to challenge you to be better, what kind of shallow friendships are they? If you are friends with someone who simply agrees with everything you do and isn't willing to move into tough conversations because they want to keep the peace, how will either of you grow?

Or worse, if all you want is a friend who never confronts you about anything because you never want to develop into anything other than what you are right now, maybe you shouldn't be friends. If that describes you, go buy a dog . . . or a robot . . . or a robot dog. It'll obey your orders.

One of the best things about bringing other people into our lives is that they challenge us to move into higher levels of maturity. Friends who are deep and lifelong have a spine and are willing to push you toward Jesus even when it's difficult to do so.

Now, let me be clear about what I'm saying here and what I'm not saying. I *am* saying that your friends should inspire you to grow and walk closer with Jesus. I am *not* saying that your friends should be domineering dictators who constantly tell you how to live your life. There is a line between deep care for someone who encourages you to live better, and a manipulative control freak who demands others to conform to their instruction. Many have crossed that line, and when it happens, bad consequences often follow, including the possible end of a friendship.

I am not telling you to constantly point out the flaws in your friends and demand they get their act together. I am not telling you to stand in judgment of your buddy's character defects and make him feel small because he isn't perfect. I am not telling you to passive-aggressively mock your sister in Christ to get her to behave the way you want her to every hour of the day. This kind of motivation for changing someone is just as sinful as the flaws you might see in them. No, please don't use what I'm saying as a license to cut down your friends.

It's important that we gently instruct our friends to walk with Jesus, but in a gentle and humble manner. When and if you decide to deliver the "wound" that Proverbs 27:6 talks about, make sure you put an ample amount of prayer into it and examine your motivations for doing so before you open your mouth and offer your instruction. Yes, the wound can hurt when it's inflicted, but if it is done without the specific purpose of helping the other person grow, irreparable damage can be done.

Many times, our friends are the best people for the job of correcting us because they are the ones who know us well enough to handle the situation with grace, discretion, and accuracy. They aren't just casual acquaintances dishing out random advice; they are true friends.

Rachael has done this well, not only now as my wife but before we were married and even before we were engaged. She has always been a wonderful example of grace and truth for me that the Lord has used in my life. She has delicately inquired about some of my anger issues, helped me process through my sinful resentment of a few events I'm required to attend for my job, and even called me out when I displayed a critical attitude. She's a great friend now, and she was a great friend before we were romantically involved. I cherish that aspect of our relationship.

Of course, it's never easy for a friend to point out your short-comings, because doing so is super scary. But real friends lean into the awkwardness and refuse to let you stay where you are, wallowing in your failures. The veneer of having it all together around your friends will not last, so let them see you, flaws and all.

And just as a side note, being an instrument of truth also needs to be timed well. A platform of trust must be built before the liberty of correction can be exercised. Going there too quickly can ruin the friendship, and you need to be careful. Use caution and wisdom, because if you don't, more harm can be created instead of less.

Is True Friendship Possible?—Reflection Questions

1. What kinds of fears from broken friendships in the past have prevented you from engaging with new relationships in the present? Be specific.

2. How is knowing "about" someone distinctly different from truly knowing someone? Explain the differences.

3. How can you be intentional about moving past the social media version of yourself among your friends and going deeper in your relationships?

10

Cultural Consumerism and Connecting with Community

Working with college students in campus ministry has its perks. Universities and campuses are often bustling epicenters of thought, activity, and ongoing social development—the perfect environment for extroverts like me. I absolutely love to spend time on college campuses, and I'm so incredibly thankful for the fact that God has allowed me to work with students over my entire vocational career.

College students are an interesting breed because they are deeply entrenched in a certain lifestyle that might seem normal to them but in reality is quite bizarre. Think about it—at no other point in life can people sleep until eleven thirty in the morning, get up and put on sweatpants, walk out into public to go get food, bring that food back to their rooms, eat it while they watch TV online, and still be considered a normal, hardworking contributor to society. It's amazing.

Those very people I just described will be running the world one day, and therein lies the main reason I love college students.

Dr. Bill Bright, the cofounder of Cru, famously said, "If you reach the college campus today, you reach the world tomorrow." I couldn't agree more, which is why I believe students at the university level are incredibly strategic at helping fulfill the Great Commission (Matthew 28:18–20).

Of course, spending significant amounts of time with this age demographic has taught me a few things about their behavioral patterns, and more specifically, the behavioral patterns of college students who are Christians. I've discovered that many well-meaning eighteen- to twenty-two-year-olds have a deep desire to connect with authentic community, yet they are very picky when it comes to church. Let me explain what I mean.

When you're a college student, nearly all of life is catered toward you. The entire experience is one long metaphorical buffet line, set up to help you achieve anything and everything you want. You get to choose your major, your classes, your roommate, your meal plan, the way you manage your time, your social interactions, your extracurricular activities, and on and on. Nearly everything at institutions of higher learning are created to maximize the student's experience.

And because of this reality, college students who follow Jesus inevitably end up thinking about church in the same way they do their evening dinner plans—as a consumer. They want to know if the menu suits their appetite for a place to attend and worship on Sunday mornings. They ask questions such as: Will I like the worship music? Is the pastor a good speaker? Are people friendly? Do I have to dress up if I go? Will I have to talk to anyone while I'm there? Do they have Wi-Fi? Are there too many people there? Is the congregation too small? Do they have a late service? Will anyone try to make me join some kind of small group?

I could keep going with the kinds of questions I've heard students ask, but the questions themselves begin to paint a certain kind of picture—a consumeristic picture. Almost every question or concern I've heard verbalized by a college student has been directly related to the idea that "church is for me." Nearly every-thing else in the lives of students aims to please, so why wouldn't they also be tempted to believe a church should do the same?

Additionally, I'd argue that this "church should meet my needs" mentality doesn't stop in the hearts of twenty-two-year-olds simply because they graduate and no longer carry student IDs. On the whole, it continues well into the next stages of life for young people (late twenties, then early thirties), and hearkens back to a root issue among many in their youth—the desire to connect with real community pitted against the simultaneous resistance to commitment.

The struggle to find authentic community in the midst of wrestling with a fear of commitment feels as if a battle is taking place inside our hearts. I, along with many people, I'm sure, want to connect with others and feel a part of a community where we belong. But the burden of committing to only one church community is often troubling to our desire to remain "free" or "unattached," much akin to our modern-day dating struggles. Commitment naturally carries a lot of baggage with it and can easily scare away a large percentage of the younger population. In his book *Why Bother with Church?*, Sam Allberry asks some of the most common questions related to church and commitment as he thinks out loud for many by saying, "There are so many reasons why we might not bother with church. Church is an effort. It is sometimes hard. And it's far from normal. So why bother going at all? Why bother making it a priority in your week, every week? Why bother getting stuck in when it means putting yourself out?"[1]

Of course, Allberry goes on to answer those questions quite well, creating a compelling case for why everyone who follows Jesus *should* bother with church, but those questions shine a rather telling spotlight on the hesitations people have concerning church involvement.

A large part of the eighteen- to thirty-five-year-old demo-graphic are asking these kinds of questions every day. They have an extremely difficult time plugging into a local church. They want to connect to a community of fellow believers, but finding the "right" church can be tantamount to finding the right e-Harmony match for some of these folks because of how they've been culturally inoculated as youths.

So what exactly is that inoculation? Well, it's the simple idea that *life is all about you.* There is an epidemic among a significant amount of American Christians that points to this reality of self-obsession, and our churches are experiencing the fallout.

I am actively involved in my local church where I live in Pennsylvania. My family and I attend Sunday morning services, I occasionally speak when our pastor needs a break, our kids are involved in the children's program, I have been on the church leadership team for six years, my wife helps to run the women's ministry, and we're both in Bible studies. Consequently, I know the inner workings of our church quite well, and I've seen with haunting regularity how people come and go from our congregation. And I'm not just talking about Sunday morning attendance either; I'm talking about folks getting involved to the degree that they're helping to run events and then dropping completely off the radar when they are confronted with something slightly disagreeable to them.

I would (kind of) like to say my church is the exception to an otherwise glowing rule, but from what I'm told by other pastors and people in ministry, it's not. In general, as soon as people find something they don't like about the churches they attend, they discard them like last year's fashion trend and move on to somewhere else. This consumeristic view of church involvement undermines the importance of plugging in to a local body of believers and reaffirms the idea that life is all about me. How sad.

Even the term "church shopping" plays off the underlying belief that a person only buys something they want to purchase because it pleases *them.* The distinct difference, of course, between buying something like a shirt and "buying" church involvement is that church involvement isn't necessarily about you. As you get involved in the natural messiness of people within the church, you realize quickly you've committed to a body of believers who aren't perfect. In fact, that body of believers is (gulp) sinful. Who wants to plug in and attach themselves to *that* if they firmly believe the church exists solely to fulfill their personal desires? Nobody.

We Are Family

I cannot change the family I was born into. My parents had me, and there is nothing I can alter about my genetic makeup, ethnicity, or DNA. My mom is my mom and my dad is my dad. I have a younger sister, and she will always be my sister regardless of how good or bad our relationship happens to be. My mother and father and sister will always be my mother and father and sister, regardless of how I treat them, how much I communicate with them, or whether or not I acknowledge they are related to me. Truth is true, and my opinion about the truth has no bearing on its truthfulness.

I am a part of a family, and it will always be that way because I can never change the makeup of that family. A coworker of mine in Cru named Byron Straughn astutely defined family this way once:

> Family is different. It's broader and deeper. Whether you're adopted or born into one, your family is responsible for your entire nurture, growth, and education. Your family is the group of people you live with and learn to love. The relationships are permanent and all-defining. Though you might be disappointed if [something like] your soccer league dissolved, you'd be devastated if your family disappeared.[2]

Byron is right. Family relationships are permanent and all-defining. So, while we might believe our relationship to church is more like a personal shopping experience (consumeristic), it is really more like a family experience (permanent and all-defining). It's incredibly important to take note of this as it relates to plugging into a community of believers within the context of church involvement and membership.

When you think of church through consumeristic eyes, jealousy can easily take hold of your heart as you hear about everything exciting that's happening in other church experiences. You can be tempted to abandon ship at your home church when you hear stories of earth-shattering sermons and rockin' worship sets elsewhere in your area. The nagging sense of buyer's remorse looms large when you believe you can find something better just up the street on a Sunday morning.

But buyer's remorse only happens in the context of a disappointing purchase and subsequent need to trade up for something shinier. If you feel as if you've been shafted on an item you've bought because it isn't living up to your expectations while your friend made a similar purchase and is loving it, inevitable jealousy will flood your life. You'll regret the purchase you've made, because this is all a natural (albeit sinful) part of the shopping experience. And if you view church through this kind of lens, something better will eventually come along and woo you to leave for the subjectively shinier option.

The natural by-product of this mind-set about church is ample amounts of stress and ambiguity. There's a constant evaluation of your church's quality standards combined with the nagging question of whether this is the best community for you to be involved with when "better options" exist out there. Commitment levels go down in the process when "leaving your options open to something better" becomes the priority. If church is all about you as a consumer, customer satisfaction reigns supreme.

A family, however, doesn't provide you this kind of license. It isn't typically viewed in the fashion I just described because families don't give someone the opportunity to experience buyer's remorse. They are what they are—namely permanent and all defining, as my friend Byron noted. As much as nearly all little kids want to trade in their brothers or sisters for someone better in the sibling category, they just can't. Through the good times and the bad, they're stuck with who they have because that's the reality of family.

There's no such thing as "trading up," "leaving your options open," or "buyer's remorse" when it comes to family, and consequently, no commitment issues about picking the "right one for me." Church involvement/membership should be more like family than shopping, and when you follow this perspective to its obvious conclusion, you'll quickly understand that it's *not* all about you.

Western thinking has tricked us into believing we should church shop until we find the perfect match for our specific tastes, and needless to say, most of American Christianity has adopted this approach. Not many view church through the lens of a family, though, and that has yielded a very specific kind of pressure.

Family has been and always will be the original community in which you belong—you were born into it or adopted into it, and it's yours. If we can dare to ascribe the family mentality to our view of the body of believers at church, the mental obstacles we have about connecting to others in that body will crumble. All of a sudden, plugging into the community is natural because our attitude about the people within the walls of the church is one of kinship. Our paradigm shift in this area can alleviate the very real troubles we have in relation to connecting with others.

Commitment

Every time the word "church" is used in the Bible, it implies a group of people and never a building;[3] therefore, we can easily infer that the people within the walls of the structure where you worship are of far greater significance to God than the bricks and mortar. In other words, (biblically speaking) when you plug in and commit to become a member of a church, you're not committing to a place, but a body of believers. And a body of believers is made up of people . . . and people are messy.

People have opinions, quirks, habits, flaws, and obsessions. People complicate things and neglect to follow through the way you want them to. People have the ability to disappoint, and they can prevent you from achieving your goals in life. People invite a certain level of chaos when they enter the picture, and the last time I checked, when it comes to chaos, nobody's really a fan.

If given a choice between the turbulence of humanity and the ability to control the environment where I worship, I'm generally going to opt for the path of least resistance, despite my desire for authentic community. People can really freak me out sometimes, and if I commit to a certain body of believers via church membership, I'm adopting the issues of that body and making them my own. Frankly, this doesn't sound too appealing, so commitment itself now becomes the object of my hesitation, preventing me from engaging fully and shouldering the responsibility of my church family. It's much easier to remain a Christian nomad, untethered to any kind of complex church body that might force me to engage with the complications of people. If I'm not committed in any kind of way, I can wash my hands of the issues a church will inevitably have and move on to where I'll be more comfortable.

But since when is the Christian life and the pursuit of godly character ever able to mature on the road laden with shortcuts? Growth is difficult. Wisdom is gained through the conduit of trials and suffering. There is no substitute for lessons learned under the gracious hand of God's discipline.

When all we do is dip our toes into the shallow end of church involvement, and then pull back when things don't align with the way we like them, we will never fully grasp the life lessons our heavenly Father has to teach us. If a fear of commitment sits in command of our church-related involvement, we'll continue in the dissatisfaction of a lonely consumer instead of a family member.

Jesus gave us the ultimate example of commitment to a flawed and messy group of people when he sacrificed himself on behalf of his friends and enemies at the cross. Since Genesis 3, humankind has been a complete disaster, fraught with one bad choice after another. Yet the God of the universe humbled himself and entered into that disaster with self-sacrificial love, forgiveness, and acceptance. In doing so, he snatched humanity away from the jaws of death, and provided the way to life everlasting. He committed himself to us in such a way that there would never be any doubt about his overwhelming love for people.

Since Christ is relentlessly committed to us, we should follow his lead by connecting and committing to a local body of believers. Jesus exhorts his followers to love one another just as he has loved us (John 13:34–35; 15:12–13), and by definition, his exhortation isn't a request. It's a command. Connection and commitment to a body of believers in a self-sacrificial way is an obedience issue, and each of us must ask the question, "Am I living obediently?"

What's My Attitude?

Young people have trouble here because culture would have them believe being invested in just one church when you're younger is tantamount to getting married right after high school. In other words, it's terrifying. But we must be diligent to fight against the temptation toward being fickle, selfish, and a loner.

Jesus gave us the example to follow when we see how he lived a life of continually giving up his rights. Listen to this description in the book of Philippians:

> Have this mind among yourselves, which is yours in Christ Jesus, who, though he was in the form of God, did not count equality with God a thing to be grasped, but

emptied himself, by taking the form of a servant, being born in the likeness of men. And being found in human form, *he humbled himself by becoming obedient* to the point of death, even death on a cross. (Philippians 2:5–8, my emphasis added)

Jesus is the Son of God. The king of the universe. When he walked the earth, he had specific rights as the king, yet he emptied himself and became obedient to the point of death on a cross. Jesus had the right to comfort, respect, justice, understanding, and life. But when we observe his life in the New Testament Gospels, we see that Jesus continually laid down his rights. He was constantly in discomfort; he was routinely disrespected; he received no justice at his trial; he was regularly misunderstood; and he was killed unfairly. Jesus embodied a life of selflessness as an example for each of us to follow.

As modern Christians (and especially Americans), we tend to do the exact opposite of what Christ did—we demand our rights. We are in the business of making our rights known, shouting it from every corner of the internet . . . and if we believe our rights have been violated in any way, we kick and scream until our demands are met in a way that satisfies us. If anyone or anything has the audacity to step on our right to comfort, respect, or justice (for example), we are completely outraged that we have been treated unfairly. And as a result of the outrage, we have grown accustomed to a belief system that feeds off of the idea that we are owed something because "my life is all about me."

But as Christians, we are not our own. Scripture says,

Or do you not know that your body is a temple of the Holy Spirit within you, whom you have from God? You are not your own, for you were bought with a price. So glorify God in your body. (1 Corinthians 6:19–20)

This means I have been purchased by God and he owns me. He owns all the rights to my life because it was a package deal when he bought me and paid for it with the blood of his only Son. The truth is I have no rights to demand because my rights aren't even mine—they're God's to do with as he pleases.

When I abandon the idea that I'm entitled to my life and it's all about me, the fear I have about certain variables such as commitment to a ministry or church begin to erode. If my life belongs to him (and according to 1 Corinthians 6, it does), I can see things in a way that help me look at a body of believers as family and not so much a product I'm purchasing as a consumer.

Sure, we want to be smart and use our God-given mind and reasoning skills to decide which church we would fit into with our personal culture, history, and talents/gifts. You need to be a part of a Bible-believing, gospel teaching and preaching body of believers. I'm not saying you should check your brain or heart at the door and become a member of the first church you attend or any church that's close to where you live.

But that is rarely the issue when it comes to connecting to a body of believers or church commitment. Much more prevalent is the American idea that "my church is about me, and if it ever steps out of line from my preferences in preaching, worship style, or even quality of coffee in the lobby, I'm out of here." This is the kind of mind-set that must stop because it fuels an attitude of entitlement.

We need to stick in a way that communicates, "even when times get tough, I'm not going anywhere. God has called me to this body of believers. He bought me with a price, and I'm all in even when it's inconvenient for me. That's what family is about, and you are my family." Strong and binding commitments like this don't fly away in the face of inconvenience or disappointment.

Cultural Consumerism and Connecting with Community—Reflection Questions

1. In what ways are you guilty of believing that church is supposed to be designed for meeting only your needs?

2. List some ways you have been a "Christian nomad," untethered to any kind of church body. What is your reasoning behind your lack of commitment?

3. Reread 1 Corinthians 6:19–20. How are you demanding your rights instead of laying them down?

11

FOMO (Fear of Missing Out)

If you're anything like me, you suffer from intermittent, mild bouts of road rage. I hate to admit this fact about myself, but the truth is the truth. Well, let me clarify. I'm not the kind of road rage guy who angrily sideswipes a minivan on the highway simply because the soccer mom behind the wheel gave me the stink-eye as she passed me on the freeway. I don't intentionally swerve to murder squirrels in the middle of the street just because they happen to be standing in the exact spot where I need to be driving. I've never intentionally cut someone off, and I've never given anyone the finger.

The best of the worst in me is truly thrust forward, however, when I sit in thick gridlocked traffic among a sea of chrome and brake lights, hoping beyond hope that around the next bend, the traffic jam will open up and I can liberally push down on the gas pedal. If my lane won't budge and the one next to me does, I always try to worm my way into that moving lane of traffic. Quite often, though, once I'm fully merged into the new lane, it will inevitably slow down and stop while the one I just left starts moving. After that, I usually end up repeatedly slamming my hands against the steering wheel like any mature adult would do.

Honestly, the whole thing is kind of embarrassing when I think about it, because regardless of which lane I use, in the end it's probably only a matter of saving or losing thirty seconds of my time. So why do I act this way? Why do I care so much? What's the fundamental issue?

I've given it some thought, and I believe it's because when I experience frustration within the lane-switching scenario I just described, I am fully immersed in the throes of FOMO. When I sit in traffic and watch the other cars around me move ahead while I stay still, FOMO has infected me to the core of my being.

FOMO (Fear of Missing Out) is a lot more than a contemporary cliché. I used it as a way to describe what I experience when I see traffic pass me by, but truthfully, it's so much more significant than just a fleeting emotion.

FOMO is now a common way of life for our modern culture and its technological advancements. We are accustomed to search engines, smartphones, and lightning-fast internet speeds, not to mention the pervading presence of social media. It has quickly become an engrained mind-set amongst all of us, filtering nearly every decision a technology-drenched person will make. And because of the wealth of information we are able to tap into at the touch of a screen living in our pockets, the fabric of our reality has been woven by the idea that other, better options are prevalent and instantly attainable.

Our world tells us, "At this very moment, you could be experiencing something better." Because we are a product of this culture, FOMO has become not just a sporadic problem to wrestle with but also a persistent reality to endure.

Sure, nearly everyone experiences the fear of missing out on better options in life from time to time. There's practically a universal anxiety that exists in an America that constantly pines for something grander, more luxurious, and more comfortable than what it currently has in front of it. Almost every advertising strategy in the nation is aimed toward the underlying urge that pulls at the average American's wallet. It's commonplace for most people to struggle with FOMO inside the course of a day, week, or month. Sad, of course, but also commonplace.

Our modern society, however, has pushed all of us far past average FOMO. We are a tech-savvy people who cannot settle for anything less than knowing all the angles in any given situation that crosses our path. As individuals, we use FOMO-inducing technologies to connect, to cope, and even to define our very existence. We digitally connect to be popular, included, and up-to-date on every social development as not to get relationally left behind.

For many millennials, a smartphone has become more than a tool to accomplish work or connect with friends. It can become a literal extension of a person, integrated into the very way we relate to and associate with the world around us.

Psychologist and author Sherry Turkle described this idea of culture's technological gadgets quite well in her TED talk when she said, "Our devices not only change what we do, but they change who we are."[1] Is this true? Yes, but only for a certain group of people.

As millennials, you aren't being altered by devices—you're growing up with them. As a generation born after the invention of the internet, you face unique challenges with technology that older generations may not encounter as intensely—simply because life as you've known it has always included these devices. It may be second nature to you to seek an instantaneous answer from Siri on your iPhone. As a generation of young men and women familiar with staying up all night waiting for the next status update, you may be tempted to "interrupt a face-to-face conversation to make sure whatever's going on elsewhere isn't better."[2] And because the steady stream of input from online surfing, social media updates, texts from friends, and app notifications constantly remind each of us of what is happening out there in the world without us, you and I have a tendency to wrestle with chronic FOMO.

Many see that it's a problem, and while we may acknowledge it, we're simply unable to stop. Psychologist and mental health researcher Dr. John Grohol notes, "[There's a] need for instant gratification and solace. Nobody can wait anymore . . . because they don't need to. After all, if you could eat all the ice cream sundaes in the world without any serious repercussions (like weight gain or being sick), why wouldn't you?"[3]

Yet even though we cannot always see them in their current form, maybe the serious repercussions are, in fact, present. Our relationship with technology and social media is still relatively new in the grand scheme of things, yet we gobble it up in large hungry mouthfuls and rarely question what it might be doing to us in the process.

As the years go by and technology increases, one thing is becoming abundantly clear—FOMO is a natural by-product of constant connection. And if it's so prolific among all people, especially within the younger generations, how should we as Christians grapple with it?

Well, the Bible tells us not to be afraid, and if we take a closer look at the life of Jesus in the New Testament, we'll be able to see that the number one command off his lips is in line with the rest of Scripture—do not fear. When the looming temptation to live in fear collides with biblical truth, however, we are left with an important problem to solve.

Will I as a follower of Jesus Christ allow the culture around me to determine how I live and behave on a daily basis, or will I choose to walk in obedience to him and define my days by a sense of peace that can only come from God himself? FOMO or peacefulness? Anxiety or serenity? True peace can only come from putting the weight of my identity and acceptance into the Lord's hands, rather than into the fickle hands of my social media connections.

The answers can appear quite obvious when we see them laid out in front of us like this, but the hour-to-hour war with FOMO can often become a living, breathing example of our fantastic ability to fail when we look at the anxiety it causes. The fear of missing out can steal your joy if you don't intentionally lean into the battle, and the realization you must come to is that FOMO itself truly makes you miss out.

The Slow Burn

It's the great irony. The fear of missing out on something actually makes you miss out on something. What is that something, you might wonder? Abundant life.

> "I came that they may have life and have it abundantly." (John 10:10)

Jesus said this. John 10:10 is his promise. A life of abundance in Christ is a pretty big "something" when you think about it, and my guess is if we truly believed that promise was under serious threat, we would fight to defend it. It's been said that if a threat is unveiled all at once, many would opt to confront that threat head on. However, if something threatening were slowly revealed in small pieces over a long period of time, most are not likely to consider that threat to be dangerous at all.

It's like the famous illustration of the frog in the pot. If you boil a pot of water and drop a frog into it, the frog will immediately jump out, but if you place tepid water and the frog in a pot at the same time and slowly heat up the water over a long period of time, the frog will stay in the pot until it dies. Morbid and disgusting? Sure, but I didn't make up the illustration. It does help to highlight my point here though.

I think if we were shown all at once what an overabundance of technology and social media usage could lead to (e.g., constant

FOMO, deterioration of authentic relationships, loss of social skills, depression, anxiety, etc.), we'd recoil in revulsion. We'd hop right out of the pot, so to speak. However, since we're fed a constant stream of technology upgrades, shiny social media platforms, and improved ways of connecting with friends, we are unable to sense the water around us getting hotter and hotter. We're boiling to death, and we don't even realize it.

Again, it's completely ironic. Because we're afraid of missing out, we immerse ourselves up to our eyeballs in a "hyper-connected" culture, yet that specific aspect of culture is drowning us in unhealthy ways of connecting. We're unable to be content in our present environment because we're so afraid something else out there might be just a little bit better than what we're currently experiencing.

A constant discontentment with the present will never lead to a life of abundance. God calls us to more than an existence of always checking our phones to see what else is going on. It's a cycle of disappointment—an ever-flowing activity of staring through the digital window at what could be better.

I've noticed while I'm driving that as I look around, people are constantly on their phones while they operate their own vehicles. Men and women on the road are risking serious injury or even death because they feel they need to know everything that's going on in the world while they drive their cars. They can't miss anything. People are essentially medicating themselves with cell phone usage, trying to avoid any bit of being left out, even for a moment. They would rather risk their own lives by texting while driving than feel alone for even a second.

There's a rampant fear of being alone, and it is affecting the way we do life. FOMO has shaped the way we communicate, the way we spend our work and free time, the way we acquire information, and certainly the way we socialize. If we aren't careful, it could seriously damage our ability to move through the necessary processes of life in a healthy way.

What to Do?

So, what can we do to prevent this damage? Well, many would argue greater connectivity or control via technology leads to greater peace and prosperity, thus expelling fear.

Modern culture says, "The ease at which people can govern the world around them and communicate with friends or family leads to a greater sense of serenity and accomplishment. The more benefits one can gain from technology, the better!"

But is that true? Maybe in a few categories; however, let's take a step back for a moment and examine something important. First, we've already talked about how more convenience can easily lead to more anxiety and FOMO, so adding additional technology to our lives to try and remove fear probably isn't the best answer. But more importantly, we must honestly ask ourselves if we believe the ideas of peace and prosperity are what will make us genuinely fulfilled or satisfied as human beings. That is the root issue.

For Christians, peace and prosperity should never be ultimate end goals. Sure, a peaceful life is the opposite of an anxious and fearful life, but if all we're willing to settle for as followers of Jesus Christ are the good gifts from God, the gifts themselves have become our end goal, not our heavenly Father. Peace and prosperity are the overflow of what it looks like to have a thriving relationship with Jesus. They are the by-product of what it means to live in harmony with the Savior of your soul. We are ultimately not in pursuit of peace and prosperity—we are after reconciliation with the Father through the blood of Jesus Christ. That reconciliation leads to the benefits of the reconciliation itself. God is peace. God is prosperity. We are in need of the Giver, not the gifts.

It's incredibly important to understand this distinction when we think about purging the fear and anxiety technology causes in our lives. If all you desire is a life of happiness, your bar is set entirely too low. Keep the main thing the main thing and aim for something greater than peace or prosperous living—pursue an intimate relationship with the One who created it all! In him alone will we find the true peace our soul thirsts after (Psalm 42:1–2).

Next, we must recognize that fear (and specifically FOMO) is really just a symptom of the greater problem within. The root of the issue lies in a mistrust of God and his goodness. When we believe life is holding out on us or that God is giving us the short end of the stick, so to speak, we'll quickly look for someone to blame. Initially in the midst of FOMO, we might accuse our friends or family for our feelings of missing out because their lives look flawless online, but when our hearts begin to connect the dots, we really just end up getting angry with God that he allowed us to be shortchanged in the first place. We've got to identify the true problem before we can begin to move on from it. FOMO exists because we believe God isn't really good. Let's begin there, and then be honest about the natural wrestling match we face on a regular basis with that false belief in our hearts. If we fail to admit the truth about the battle within, we'll never be able to break free of the bond anxiety and fear have over us.

Lastly, we must trust the Lord with our anxieties about tomorrow. We can't let the fear and anxiety we have about tomorrow compound the complexity of today.[4] Jesus tells us in Matthew 6:34, "Therefore do not be anxious about tomorrow, for tomorrow will be anxious for itself. Sufficient for the day is its own trouble."

If I've got an event, for example, coming up in the days ahead that tempts me to fear, it will do me no good today if I worry about the event in the future. In fact, all it will do is sour my current reality. I don't need to worry myself with the potential problems of that event, because God is already there, and he and I will deal with it together when the time comes. I must not be anxious about tomorrow.

If I'm worried that by committing to one opportunity now I might be missing out on a better option that might come along afterward (FOMO), I will live in a constant fear and second-guessing of my decisions. The fear of missing out is largely fueled by the "what if," and the mind-set of "what if" can put my life into a perpetual state of anxiety about the future. How miserable!

Let me fill you in on something: life is going to be full of both wonderful and terrible things. The sum of your days will have a mixture of difficulties and pleasures. Pain is inevitable. Joy is inevitable. However, living in fear today of what those unpredictable days tomorrow will hold is folly. Jesus asks in Matthew 6:27 if anyone can add a single hour to his lifespan by worrying, and the implication is most definitely, "no."

So take heart. Jesus is with you today, and when/if the difficult times come tomorrow, he won't abandon you then either. There is no need to fill up today with anxiety about what could happen in the days to come. If you miss out on something tomorrow, it isn't really all that bad. In fact, I'd be willing to say if you're walking with God and remaining sensitive to the Holy Spirit's lead over your life, there's really no such thing as missing out. How can you miss out on something better when the One who directs your life is proactively shaping your paths (Proverbs 3:5–6)? You can't.

Give any anxiety you have about the possible future over to him right now and watch the FOMO you wrestle with evaporate from your heart. Placing your trust in God Almighty, the Creator of heaven and earth, is a regret nobody will ever experience.

Fomo (Fear of Missing Out)—Reflection Questions

1. How have you used technology to connect, cope, and even define who you are as a person? In what ways has that technology created more FOMO in your heart?

2. How has FOMO personally robbed you of the abundant life Jesus talks about in John 10:10?

3. Have peace and prosperity become your goals for life? In what ways have you pursued the gifts of God over God himself?

12

Dealing with Enemies

In light of the fact that I'm short and have been so since as far back as I can remember, this was the particular thing about me people chose to make fun of when I was coming up through grade school. Now, I know practically everyone has their thing that other people mocked when they were younger, so I'm not trying to single out my issue and make it more significant than what you may have gone through. But the past is written all the same, and I can't deny people made fun of me a lot when I was a kid.

I wouldn't say, however, that I was *bullied* for being little. But as I've already noted in an earlier chapter, as a military kid I never stayed in one place for too long, so with each move to a new school, I'd encounter a fresh set of insults from anyone who wanted to make himself feel superior to me.

One year in particular, my transition from fifth grade in Guam to sixth grade in Virginia, proved to be more difficult than usual. Middle school is middle school, and it's awkward for almost everyone, but being the new kid compounds the hardship all the more. For the first two months of sixth grade, I experienced repeated ridicule from a group of three other guys who counted it their daily duty to point out the fact that I was short.

It obviously bothered me and made me feel insignificant, so I eventually went in to see the school's guidance counselor in an attempt to acquire some help, or at the very least, advice on what I should do. Now, this appointment was a long time ago for me, but strangely enough, I can vividly remember exactly what that guidance counselor said to me in her office the day I went in to seek her assistance.

"Kill 'em with kindness," she said. "When they are mean to you, you be nice right back to them."

This wasn't the type of guidance I expected to get from her that day, but the truth is it was probably the best thing she could have said to me. I applied her recommendation immediately. When my three adversaries said something cruel to me in the hallway during the class switch that afternoon, I remember commenting about how much I genuinely liked one of their shirts. They had no idea how to respond, and simply laughed at me as a group before sitting down in our next class. I kept it up though, and complimented all three of them every chance I got. And wouldn't you know it, I killed their mockery with kindness. It only took about three days of countering their maliciousness with courteousness, and not one of those guys ever said anything harsh to me ever again. Actually, one of the guys, Mike, ended up being a really funny guy and a good friend of mine until I moved again a few years later.

I know this story isn't super dramatic, mirroring the plot of some young adult novel set in the context of a Hollywood high school, but nonetheless, for those first two months of sixth grade, I considered those three boys my enemies. I hated their treatment of me, and by extension, I hated them. I wanted all three of them to be cut down to the level they made me feel every time they ridiculed me. I wanted to fire back insults at them, making light of their intellect, their fashion choices, or their hygiene. I wanted them to feel low, the way I felt low, so I could pay them back for every slur they made at my expense. I wanted justice.

Naturally, I was more than a bit surprised when my guidance counselor told me I should do the exact opposite. Perhaps that's why I didn't wait to implement her suggestion and paid them compliments instead of insults—its radicalness jarred me and instantly made me feel like it would work. I knew in my heart of hearts that it was wrong to return evil for evil. The captivating nature of goodness drew me in and quenched my hate.

For the Bible Tells Me So

Many years later when I became a Christian during my freshman year of college at Virginia Tech, I ran across this teaching of Jesus when he said, "You have heard that it was said, 'You shall love your neighbor and hate your enemy.' But I say to you, Love your enemies and pray for those who persecute you, so that you may be sons of your Father who is in heaven" (Matthew 5:43–45).

And then again by the apostle Paul in Romans when he says,

> Bless those who persecute you; bless and do not curse them. . . . Repay no one evil for evil, but give thought to do what is honorable in the sight of all. If possible, so far as it depends on you, live peaceably with all. Beloved, never avenge yourselves, but leave it to the wrath of God, for it is written, "Vengeance is mine, I will repay, says the Lord." To the contrary, "if your enemy is hungry, feed him; if he is thirsty, give him something to drink; for by so doing you will heap burning coals on his head." Do not be overcome by evil, but overcome evil with good. (Romans 12:14, 17–21)

The way the Bible so eloquently describes it is very much along the lines of "kill 'em with kindness." Of course, Jesus and Paul say it much better than my guidance counselor did all those years ago, but I think you get my point. When we are tempted toward hatred of our enemies because of who they are or what they've done, the biblical exhortation speaks to the opposite and tells us to repay their evil with blessing. Put a stop to the endless cycle of payback and forgive as the Lord has forgiven us.

The idea of forgiveness can certainly be a difficult pill to swallow, especially when we've been sinned against over and over again. Frankly, sometimes it's just easier to hate someone. But what makes us different as Christians is the very cornerstone of our faith—we are a forgiven people. It's our identity. It's who we are at the core of our being. We have been forgiven by God through Jesus Christ, and as his followers, we are called to be like him and forgive others (Ephesians 4:32).

As people of forgiveness (both receiving and extending) we exude the light of Christ to a dark and cynical world, drawing people toward the Savior, and prompting them to scratch their heads in bewilderment as to why we don't pay people back when they deserve punishment from us. Forgiveness and grace are never the default of an unbelieving, sinful heart, so when we forgive, we provide tangible evidence of a renewed and reconciled life where God has been at work, changing us from within (2 Corinthians 5:16–21).

It's what all believers have in common. Seminary professor and Reformed Evangelical theologian D. A. Carson puts it well stating,

> The reason there are so many exhortations in the New Testament for Christians to love other Christians is because . . . the church itself is not made up of natural "friends." It is made up of natural enemies. What binds us together is not common education, common race, common income levels, common politics, common nationality, common accents, common jobs, or anything else of that sort [that bind most other groups of people together]. Christians come together not because they form a natural collocation, but because they have all been saved by Jesus Christ

and owe him a common allegiance. In this light we are a band of natural enemies who love one another for Jesus' sake. That is the only reason why John 13:34–35 makes sense when Jesus says: "A new command I give you—love one another as I have loved you." Christian love will stand out and bear witness to Jesus because it is a display, for Jesus' sake, of mutual love among social incompatibles.[1]

We are different and remarkably attractive to a world that constantly craves an eye for an eye. Non-believers simply don't understand unmerited favor and the cancellation of any kind of debt owed to another person. It's what makes us so unique because it's a reflection of the unique Jesus of Nazareth—a man who loved his enemies and prayed for their forgiveness at the very moment he was being crucified because of their hatred of him (Luke 23:34).

By the power of the Holy Spirit who lives inside of us, we have the supernatural ability to extend forgiveness not only to the ones we love and like, but to our enemies as well. And in the process, earthly relationships can be restored while God gets the glory.

Undoubtedly, this can be harder with some who have deeply wounded us, either once or in a repetitive way. I know I have certainly failed to love those in my life who have atrociously wronged me, because forgiveness is always extremely costly. There have been many times in my life when I have not wanted to pay the price and suffer to extend forgiveness. But if I'm unwilling to suffer for the cost of grace, I'm neglecting to appreciate the suffering Jesus went through on my behalf. Pastor and author Tim Keller puts it well when he says,

And if we can't forgive without suffering, how much more must God suffer in order to forgive us? If we unavoidably sense the obligation and debt and injustice of sin in our soul, how much more does God know it? On the cross we see God forgiving us, and that was possible only if God suffered. On the cross God's love satisfied his own justice by suffering, bearing the penalty for sin. There is never forgiveness without suffering, nails, thorns, sweat, blood. Never.[2]

Forgiveness is suffering, and if God was willing to do it on behalf of all humanity, I should be willing to do it too because I directly benefit from his grace and forgiveness (Colossians 3:13). Without God's forgiveness, relationship with him wouldn't ever be possible. The fracture that was made because of our sin wouldn't ever be repaired, and the state of mankind would be utterly hopeless.

But the Lord does forgive. The gospel is true, and we are alive because of Christ's atoning work on the cross. Forgiveness has been extended to us, and that forgiveness is truly our only hope.

When we rest in the safety and comfort of the gospel, absorbing the full benefits of his kind extension of forgiveness toward us, we are compelled to spread compassion to others who have wronged us. We cripple the glory of the gospel in the world's eyes when we fail to forgive, and we magnify the gospel's glory when we develop a lifestyle of offering grace and mercy not only to our friends but our enemies as well.

Dealing with Enemies—Reflection Questions

1. How can both receiving and extending forgiveness be a proclamation of the gospel in your life to those who don't know Christ?

2. How has it been hard for you to extend forgiveness instead of vengeance to those who have wronged you?

3. We forgive because we have been forgiven. List the compelling ways the gospel convinces you to forgive both your friends and your enemies.

The Pressure Because of Difficulty

Section 3 will help you navigate many of the hurdles you encounter as a student. Being a follower of Jesus Christ can sometimes add an extra wrinkle of complexity as you think about all the preexisting "normal" troubles a student has to deal with in college from the get-go. In light of that, we're going to talk about answers to common questions we may have from the standpoint that the Bible speaks directly and intentionally to us when we ask. We're going to process difficult subjects Christians uniquely deal with and not shy away from the anxiety they may cause in our hearts. We've already discussed the pressures that come as we talk about our life's purpose and our relationships with other people. This section will help guide you through the inevitable complexities of walking with God while you come face-to-face with trials. Suffering well now as a student can be an invaluable tool for facing suffering in the future because it prepares and refines you in a way nothing else can.

13

Immediate Success and Depth of Character

Patience is not a virtue of mine. In fact, I remember thinking at one point not too long ago, "I'm a pretty impatient person and I should probably pray for patience . . . but then God will put me in situations where I'll have to be patient, and I don't think I want that at all." I know, I know, I'm such a great model of wisdom and spirituality, huh?

Yet while I'm somewhat embarrassed about this, I don't think I'm alone in my impatience. Look at what the insightful author and leadership guru Simon Sinek had to say in a recent interview about young people:

> They have grown up in a world of instant gratification. You want to buy something? You go on Amazon and it shows up the next day. You want to get in touch with someone? You don't leave a message on their machine and wait four hours for them to get the message; you just text them and they get back to you immediately. Want to watch a movie? You just log on and watch it; you don't have to check movie times. Everything happens in an instant.

You want to get a date? Swipe right. You don't even have to muster up the courage to [ask someone out]. And so the problem is [young people] are accused of being entitled. I don't think they're entitled at all. I think they're impatient . . . it's as if they see the summit as they're standing at the foot of a mountain. They can see the summit (the thing they want)—what they don't see is the mountain . . . this large immoveable object. You can go up fast or go up slow, but there's still a mountain. What they don't understand is that life, relationships, and career fulfillment are a journey. There's no app for that.[1]

Many of the college students and young professionals I interact with would, in my observation, align with what Sinek is describing here. They are incredibly idealistic about life and making an impact in the world, but if that impact doesn't happen in the short period of time they are used to because of their immersion in technology and indoctrination of instant gratification, they can become quickly frustrated and move on to something new in their desire to change the world. They generally want immediate success, but as Sinek points out, life is a journey . . . and journeys take time.

Slow Cooked

In our culture today, immediacy is the name of the game. It's everywhere around us: the speed of the internet, overnight delivery, Hot Pockets, and the like. Most people assume that if you can't get it quick, it pretty much isn't worth getting at all. This is one reason the credit card industry is doing so well—get it now, pay for it later. Instant gratification.

I guess this is why the things that move slowly in this world stand in such graphic contrast to the haste of their surrounding environment. Handwriting a letter, for example, is a rarity when people open their mailboxes nowadays. I know I'm personally taken by surprise when I'm blessed enough to get one. Moreover, if a meal takes longer than thirty minutes to prepare, we often skip that recipe when we flip through a cookbook or click through ideas on Pinterest.

And since time-occupying habits like this are so uncommon in the modern world we live in, they often have an effect on us that we are unable to ignore. Case in point: Thanksgiving dinner is always worth talking about because it usually takes all day to prepare. Or gloating when you finish reading a one-thousand-page novel becomes inevitable because it probably takes triple the time to read in comparison to the average book. In short, the more time, the more noteworthy and influential. Those who are savvy know this.

A friend of a friend of mine started up a restaurant in Orlando, Florida (the chain restaurant capital of the world), specializing in slow-cooked pork barbecue. He goes to painstaking lengths to make sure the food he serves is quality meat, cooked slowly over an absurd amount of time. Why? Because when it's cooked slower, it tastes better. And his deliberate choices in barbecue preparation have paid off in spades. Every day, there is a line out the door from when they open to when they close. People are willing to wait in line for that slow-cooked pork barbecue in 98-degree weather with 100 percent humidity because they know they are getting a delicious, quality, tasty product. There is no substitute for the element of time.

While immediate success might be something most young people long for because it's what they are used to, that simply isn't how authentic, rich, wholesome, satisfying life works. As Simon Sinek points out, "There's no app for that."

It has taken me a while to define myself in this way, but when people ask me what I do for a living, I often describe myself as an author. I've written books for a number of years now, but when I first graduated from college, I had no aspirations of becoming an author. In fact, I was a full-time missionary with Cru for ten years before I even started to write. God used the first decade of ministry experience in my life to work on me and give me something to say before I was even able to write anything of significance.

What's my point? Well, the good things in life often take time. There is no substitution for character, and character in a person is almost always born in the crucible of time. Character cannot be rushed, and to try and do so is futile. This is important to understand in light of success, because success without character can lead to dangerous and destructive places. Think about all of the people who became successful at a young age, and then experienced the inevitable fallout as a result because of a lack of character in their lives. Justin Bieber, Lindsay Lohan, Britney Spears, Drew Barrymore, Amanda Bynes, and Macaulay Culkin are just a few examples of young kids thrust into the spotlight of fame and success, only to then show they were unable to deal with it in one form or fashion by turning to alcohol, drugs, and even vandalism. Why? Because they were just kids when they got famous, and character in a person simply takes time to develop.

Making wise choices implies the character quality of wisdom, and as we read the Bible, we can see that true wisdom comes from the Lord.

> For *the* Lord *gives wisdom*; *from his mouth* come *knowledge* and *understanding*; he stores up sound wisdom for the upright; he is a shield to those who walk in *integrity*, guarding the paths of justice and watching over the way of his saints. Then you will understand righteousness and justice and equity, every good path; for *wisdom* will come into your heart, and *knowledge* will be pleasant to your soul; *discretion* will watch over you, *understanding* will guard you, *delivering you* from the way of evil, from men of perverted speech, who forsake the paths of uprightness to walk in the ways of darkness, who rejoice in doing evil and delight in the perverseness of evil, men whose paths

are crooked, and who are devious in their ways. (Proverbs 2:6–15, my emphasis added)

This is only one example of many in Scripture (and in particular, the book of Proverbs) when the Bible talks about the extreme benefits of wisdom. It's an incredibly valuable attribute in a person. Proverbs even goes as far to say it is "life for your soul" (3:21–22). But again, wisdom comes from the Lord, and God usually provides said wisdom over a long period of time, not in an instant.

All Christians are called to walk with God, and walking consists of slow, steady steps of progression that a person can keep up in a sustained way over a long period of time. Walking is not running. It is not jumping ahead. Walking takes time. Knowing and understanding this in our hearts will help alleviate the temptation to yearn for immediate success, immediate results, and instant gratification. There have been no shortcuts to my growth toward getting wisdom in the many years I have been a Christian, and there will be no shortcuts to yours either. Let me add a little to what I've already stated: there is no substitute for the *soul-sanctifying* element of time.

We've Gone Digital

I am old enough to remember a time when internet access wasn't always available everywhere I went. In fact, when I would visit my parents during a winter or spring break in college, I went completely without internet because my folks didn't have it in their home at the time. It always felt like a step backward when I wasn't able to gain access to information I was completely used to getting anytime I wanted when I was on campus. You get accustomed to a certain speed when it comes to convenience or information access, and when the speed decreases, frustration can abound.

Similarly, when God is perhaps orchestrating events in your life for the purpose of slowing you down, no doubt your first inclination will be disgruntlement. You're probably used to things moving so quickly in your world that any time life seems to be "loading," the pace is unbearably sluggish. But what if instead of frustration your response was that of faithfulness? What if you leaned into the unhurried pace the Lord was setting for you and trusted him as you weren't immediately successful? What if you truly believed there was no substitute for the soul-sanctifying element of time?

Nehemiah waited four months before taking action after hearing his home (Jerusalem) lay in ruins (Nehemiah 1). Jacob waited for over fourteen years to marry Rachel, the woman he loved (Genesis 29). The apostle Paul studied for three years after his conversion before beginning his ministry (Galatians 1:18). Abraham waited twenty-five years for the promised birth of his heir Isaac (Genesis 21). For crying out loud, Joseph was sold into slavery when he was seventeen years old, and the resolution/reconciliation with his brothers didn't happen until he was thirty-nine (Genesis 45)—that's twenty-two years of ambiguity! And on and on it goes in Scripture.

In fact, when you think about it, all of time itself has been about waiting. Since the fall in Genesis 3, humanity has been waiting for the ultimate crushing of the serpent's head (Genesis 3:15) when Christ returns to conquer the evil one (Revelation 20), which has already happened, and not yet happened. Or as one author put it, "Satan's defeat occurred two thousand years ago; his final doom is certain."[2]

Simply put, God uses waiting. Immediate success doesn't build character, integrity, or depth in a human being because patiently waiting on the Lord does. When we respond to waiting with aggravation, we just might be missing out on God's best plan for us. Slow might be bad when it comes to Wi-Fi speeds and software downloads, but slow in the biblical sense is an avenue toward maturity and depth in Christ. Maybe it's time to take a breather and examine where God wants you to slow down that he might sanctify you more into the image of his Son.

Immediate Success and Depth of Character
Reflection Questions

1. Reread Psalm 27:14. How has the element of time helped you gain character and wisdom? Where have you been tempted to take shortcuts on the road to wisdom/character?

2. How has immediate success with something in your past actually had a negative effect in your life?

3. Where is God currently asking you to wait?

14

Spiritual Warfare

For the better part of the last decade, my wife and I have had the privilege and honor of leading a summer mission project in Ocean City, Maryland. The mission team is made up of around thirty-five college students and fifteen Cru staff from all over the country, running from mid-May to early August each year in the little beach town.

The summer-long event is kind of like spiritual boot camp. I tell the students on the first day that we as the staff overlap with them for five weeks, then we pass the leadership of the mission off to them once we leave. Consequently, there's not much time to fool around—we mean business. I unashamedly tell them I have five weeks to prepare them for the next fifty years, and I take that responsibility very seriously.

Students have to go through an application process, get references, and raise a few thousand dollars to attend. Once they arrive, they get a local job to work during the days, and at night the schedule is filled with spiritually enriching activities, such as stepping out in boldness to share their faith on the boardwalk, Bible study, times of corporate prayer, outreach to international students in the area, discipleship meetings with staff, and much more all while living together in one house made up of four different apartments. In my opinion, it's the best thing Cru has to offer to college students who want to grow in their faith, learn how to share the gospel, and gain hearts for the world.

Naturally, the time is pretty intense, so it can be very draining on me and the staff who run it during the first part of the summer. Each year, my family picks up and moves to Ocean City, living away from our home for the better part of the summer season. It's crazy, but we love it.

And with the focus of sharing the gospel while we're on the mission, I've been no stranger to what I could only describe as spiritual attack each year. Annoying operational hindrances, unique conflict with my wife, personal health issues, and frequent bouts of unusual anxiety have been the name of the game for me in both preparation for the mission and while on-site in Maryland.

In fact, one summer after only a few days in town, I found myself bolting upright in bed in the middle of the night with an eerie feeling of dread that the mission was hated by numerous people in town and we were destined to be shut down and kicked out of our housing because of our opposition to the darkness by spreading the gospel. I was overwhelmed by the thought that the enemy did not want us there doing what we were doing, and he was dead set on making the mission fail.

After I processed that experience with both my wife and our staff team the next day, we all prayed fervently that as we did battle with the spiritual forces that opposed us, we would lean wholeheartedly on the truth of God's Word and the power of his Holy Spirit to do wondrous things in the lives of our students on the mission, our lives as staff, and the hearts of the lost in town. God works powerfully each year in Ocean City, but that year in particular, more gospel presentations were heard and more of our students committed to going overseas to serve the Lord than ever before. I don't believe that was a coincidence.

The Threat Is Real

Now, I'm not what you might label as a Christian who ascribes every trouble or trial to a specific spiritual attack. I don't usually say a demon is responsible for my fender bender, or the bad weather is a spiritual sign I'm not supposed to go outside and share my faith today. Some people I know are like that, and I'm not knocking it at all, but I simply don't think I need to pray against the demonic attack of materialism every time I go to Target.

However, the Bible is very clear that an unseen battle is going on. Paul says in Ephesians, "Put on the whole armor of God, that you may be able to stand against the schemes of the devil. For we do not wrestle against flesh and blood, but against the rulers, against the authorities, against the cosmic powers over this present darkness, against the spiritual forces of evil in the heavenly places" (Ephesians 6:11–12).

I may not be aware of it, but a war is happening all around me, and to ignore it is foolishness. In verse thirteen and following, Paul goes on to describe the specifics of our readiness and how we should prepare for the reality of this cosmic fight. When you want to honor God and make choices in your life to walk with him by putting off your old self, the evil one hates it, and he hates you too. Expect opposition.

In my years of ministry, so many students have asked me why it's so difficult to walk with God when all they want to do is live a life that's pleasing to him.

You might ask, "If I'm pursuing a life that's pleasing to God, why doesn't he make things easier?" The question seems logical, but following Christ is never a life of ease. In fact, Jesus himself promises hardship when he says, "I have said these things to you, that in me you may have peace. In the world you will have tribulation. But take heart; I have overcome the world" (John 16:33).

Tribulation comes both from the world (John 15:18–19), and from the evil one (Ephesians 6:16), and Jesus communicates that it is inevitable. It will happen. Don't anticipate a life of comfort just because you're a Christian, expect just the opposite. Why? Because once you become a follower of Christ, you are no longer a citizen of this world. God has bought you with a price (1 Corinthians 6:19–20; 7:23), and the cost was his very own Son. You have been plucked from the kingdom of darkness and are now a citizen of heaven, currently living in a world that does not identify with your citizenship. The world and the forces of evil are hostile toward your citizenship, looking for ways to tear it apart, slow it down, and make it stop.

Naturally then, things are not going to be easy when you stand up for God and his principles. Things will be difficult and troublesome, so the more we understand and prepare for that truth, the better.

And just as an aside: Yes, life is hard as a follower of Christ, but the hardship is 100 percent worth it. A pastor friend of mine once said, "Coming to Jesus does not remove all your troubles. In fact when you come to him, you may discover many more troubles than you once had. But you also discover that Jesus is faithful to walk with you through them. And that makes every trial worth enduring."[1] Such great perspective. As a Christian, a life of trials is a life with Jesus, and life with him is always better than life without him.

He Has Overcome

Sometimes we can have a tendency with all of this to overcompensate and become somewhat obsessive about the spiritual battle, dwelling on it day and night. This happened to me in my early years of following Christ, and quite frankly, I became irrationally fearful of Satan and his minions, believing a demon was around every corner waiting to attack me because I was now a Christian.

We want to be aware of the very real battle going on in the spiritual realm, but not ascribe more power to the opposition than they have in reality. Remember the words of Jesus that he has overcome the world. Don't forget that any time Jesus had a run-in with an evil spirit of any kind, they trembled before him and needed to ask permission to do anything (Mark 5:1–20; Luke 8:26–39). The powers of darkness have never and will never be stronger than the Son of God. "Little children, you are from God and have overcome them, for he who is in you is greater than he who is in the world" (1 John 4:4).

The victory belongs to Jesus, so it's important to live as though we actually believe that and not give more attention to the enemy than is due. Don't overly obsess about the darkness, but don't ignore the darkness either. A healthy middle ground is appropriate here, where we acknowledge the spiritual battle but don't consume ourselves with it.

Spiritual Warfare—Reflection Questions

1. To what extreme have you leaned toward in the past—ignoring spiritual battle or obsessing over it?

2. Reread both accounts of Jesus's interaction with the demon Legion in Mark 5:1–20 and Luke 8:26–39. List the ways Jesus has total authority over the demons/spiritual realm.

3. Do you expect a life of ease or comfort because you are a follower of Christ? Examine your heart and list some of your expectations of God in light of the fact that you're a Christian. Now give those expectations to the Lord and rest in his good plan for your life, whatever it may bring.

15

Peer Evaluation

When my oldest daughter, Quinn, was approaching the end of her kindergarten year, it was announced in a newsletter from her elementary school that they would be throwing their first annual daddy-daughter dance. Needless to say, this was a big deal in the Abbott household.

We put the date on the calendar and counted down until the dance arrived. And when we reached the big day, my wife and I decided to do it up right. Quinn put on a really cute dress, wore jewelry for the second time in her life, and even applied some makeup to her face (with Rachael's help, of course). I wore the nicest clothes in my closet, got a fresh haircut, and even stopped by a real flower shop—not a grocery store—to buy Quinn a bouquet of flowers that was more expensive than most of the textbooks I purchased during my freshman year of college. But she was worth it.

When my daughter and I got to her school, we waited in line to fill out this little form to enter for a door prize and I could hear the blaring music thumping down the hallway that led to the gym. After answering a few questions on the form about my favorite color, Quinn and I walked through the double doors toward the sound of an old Justin Bieber song, and I was shocked by what I saw in the room. All of the school's kindergarten through fifth-grade girls were in the middle of the gym, jumping and dancing around to the music while every single father lined the outside perimeter of the room, staring at their daughters.

It was like a middle school dance! Literally none of the dads were dancing with their kids. The segregation in the room was so obvious that my little five-year-old said, "Daddy, I think you're supposed to stand over with all the other dads while I go dance."

I crouched down, looked Quinn in the eyes, and said, "No, sweetie. Do you want to dance with me?" She nodded, so I took both of her hands in mine and we waded into the sea of little jumping girls to start dancing.

I'll never forget that moment, because as I led Quinn out into the middle of the gym floor, all the daughters looked at me with smiles while all the fathers looked at me with terror on their faces. I could tell none of the dads were innately comfortable with the idea of dancing in front of a room of other men. But at the very least, I was a catalyst for change because once I broke the ice as the first father to hit the dance floor, quite a few other dads joined in and the rest of the night was truly a beautiful thing for everyone in attendance. We danced the night away, which is to say we danced until seven-thirty p.m. and made it home in time for Quinn to get in her pajamas and into bed before eight-fifteen.

As I recall this story, I can vividly remember the feeling I had in my gut when my gaze scanned the perimeter of the room and every father's eyes were on me. There was a split second when this intense feeling of insecurity punched me in the stomach, and I wanted to retreat because I felt odd and judged by them. But thankfully that feeling quickly went away because I remembered why I was truly at the dance that night. My singular goal was to please my little girl and show her the best time I could at the daddy-daughter dance. Once I remembered my purpose, the insecurity vanished, and we both had a fantastic time.

Approval Culture

In an interview conducted by Tony Reinke on the Desiring God website, teen author Jaquelle Crowe was asked about the connection between pervasive smartphone use among teens and the coinciding damaging emotional effects. Here's what she had to say:

> Smartphones contribute significantly to the 24-7 approval culture we live in. There's no escaping it. This is something our parents don't always understand, because when they were teenagers, that culture was largely limited to the 9–3 school day . . . But now there's 24-7 social media. There's a constant comparison and peer approval game that cannot be escaped. And it's crippling, exhausting, and undeniably stressful. You can't get away from the likes, the shares, the texts, the pictures. It's like the popularity contest never ends. And it works both ways. Your smartphone gives you a front-row seat to watch the popularity contest, too.[1]

There's an undeniable reality that our culture today will not allow most to escape its ever-evaluating eyes. Sure, you could live off the grid away from technology and communication, but most young people have never considered that possibility, let alone tried it to see what life would be like. Consequently, most people are online in one form or fashion, and if you're out there in cyberspace, you can and most likely will be seen and critiqued. This may not seem too bad, but as Jaquelle Crowe points out, the internet doesn't take a break, so the approval game cannot be escaped. And with the constant pressure of peer evaluation and popularity contests, a significant amount of young men and women buckle under the weight of such socio-digital stress.

Sure, many won't break beneath the weight of public digital opinion as they live their lives online, but I don't think anyone is immune to a desire for approval. We were created by God to connect in community, and if there is no feeling of connection, insecurity will creep in and start us on a pattern of searching for approval in any and every way we can get it.

No doubt you've met someone at one point in your life and thought, *Geez, that girl is insecure. All she does is try to get everyone around her to validate who she is and approve of what she does.* Admit it, you've thought that about someone before. Sure, it might seem super judgmental, but the truth is we're all looking for the validation of others because we're all exactly the same. We're all insecure.

And while it might be considerably obvious to spot such a characteristic in someone when his behavior reflects it out in the real world, everything starts to get more and more subtle when we haul our insecurity onto the digital platform.

One summer many years ago before smartphones were invented, I was on a summer mission with a few dozen college students and about twelve Cru staff. While we were there, one guy on the mission was in the habit of taking self-portraits with a little point-and-shoot digital camera and then uploading them to Facebook on an almost daily basis. At the time, his behavior in my mind was incredibly odd because it felt narcissistic and consequently insecure.

I remember wondering, "Why on earth would someone take picture after picture of his own face and post it online for other people see?"

Naturally, it was easy for me to observe this in his life, and then talk to him about why he felt the need to do something that continually pointed to his need for validation. We were able to dialogue about his insecurity, and as he surrendered it over to the Lord, I believe he grew a lot in that area over the summer.

My oh my, I'd have a lot more trouble with that kind of conversation today, wouldn't I? What seemed so odd a few years ago is now a completely normal and socially acceptable form of social media, communication, and self-expression in the world of 24-7 selfies. It's almost bizarre if you can't figure out what people look like as you scroll through their Instagram feeds. Taking pictures of ourselves is now the primary way we catalog our lives and show people how we're feeling, who we're with, where we've been, and what we're doing. If you can't find a selfie among a person's social media portfolio, something seems off and a bit strange about that person.

And therein lies my point. What seemed weird before is now the complete opposite in our modern culture, leaving room for the insecurities of life to not only hide behind our online presence, but pridefully masquerade as self-esteem. You can't really tell the difference these days between an insecure person and an arrogant one because the internet is constantly providing outlets for self-expression, self-adoration, self-confidence, self, self, self. And the ironic thing is that most of the people who appear to have it all together online are often the most insecure. Social media has simply given them the opportunity to bury their insecurities under a pile of humble-brag posts and filtered selfies. As I stated earlier, our struggle with insecurity is much more subtle when we transcribe our lives onto the digital platform.

Additionally, it's hard to simply quit. According to research by Dr. Nancy Cheever at California State University, social media and phone-induced anxiety operate on a positive feedback loop. She says phones keep us in a persistent state of anxiety, and the only relief from this anxiety is to look at our phones.[2] However, as followers of Jesus Christ, we can see that the gospel teaches us just the opposite about where to find relief.

Our Relief

We find our relief from life's pressures—measuring up to others, the weight of insecurity, the anxiety of social media—in the life, death, and resurrection of God's Son. Relief from the strain of the digital world doesn't come by absorbing more of the digital world—that's ridiculous! That's like when someone tries to cure his hangover in the morning with a beer and a shot of whiskey.

Scripture clearly points out that God was willing to pay the ultimate sacrifice for us, and as a result, nothing can separate us from his love (Romans 8:31–39). What if we lived as if we actually believed what the Bible says is true of us? What if we stood firm on the certainty that nothing could ever separate us from the love of God in Christ Jesus our Lord (Romans 8:39)? Do you think we would find authentic relief? Do you think we would wrestle as much with insecurity?

The evaluation of our peers shouldn't ever be the measuring tool of our worth because the Bible is clear about how much value we hold. We're apparently worth the value of Christ's shed blood, and having faith in him alters our perspective altogether for his glory.

Peer Evaluation—Reflection Questions

1. How have you specifically felt the pressure of online peer evaluation and popularity contests?

2. Where do you turn to relieve the stress from life's pressures? Do those avenues bring more or less insecurity to your life?

3. After a close examination of your heart, do you find that faith or insecurity is ruling your life?

16

Where Is Jesus in the Hard Times?

I recently led a large group of Christian college students through an intentional learning exercise one evening designed to keep them ignorant about the point of the experience until the very end of the night during a debriefing time. And because of the nature of the exercise, some of the students leaned toward an extreme emotional response. By that I mean a few of the students got really ticked off.

We played a game that divided the group up into teams and asked everyone to work together for a specific purpose. Each group had a board game-style map, some dice, little characters to move around the board, and challenges to read. The goal was for the group to attain as much treasure as possible in the time period allotted, but they needed to work together and think outside the box on how gaining treasure could be done most effectively.

Naturally, when you divide a group up into teams, the competitive spirit takes over, and they think working as a team means just their small team. Everyone thinks it's about getting treasure for their specific group, and not the group as a whole. Consequently, the other teams in the room become the enemy and not allies. In the end, they learn that if they would have worked together as one big group of players instead of individual teams, they would have gained ten times the amount of treasure as a collective.

It's always a bit risky to mask your real intentions when putting a group of people through an elaborate game like I did that evening, because the reaction can be anger-inducing. Personally, however, I'll take a reaction over indifference any day, so when some of the students got mad because they felt deceived by the game, I wasn't too bent out of shape over their anger.

I'll admit part of the process was gathering everyone's phones at the beginning of the time so they had to communicate by talking with one another instead of texting, coupled with slowly turning up the heat in the room too in order created tension. Consequently, I didn't really blame them for getting upset.

Some of the students told me they didn't like the experience because they felt as if they were intentionally led through something that made them feel uncomfortable and uneasy. One student complained to me afterward that she "felt like we were being tortured." Sure, there was a lack of modern-day comfort during the experience, but at no time was anyone's health in danger. I promise nobody was tortured.

The debriefing time at the end did wonders to help everyone involved learn about what the point of the evening was all about, and it assuaged most of the reactive negative emotion. However, the one student's comment about feeling as if she was being tortured really stuck with me in the days following the learning exercise. Did she genuinely experience misery, torment, or suffering through this one little event, or was her response to it an overreaction caused by unmet expectations about how she thought the world should operate? My guess was it was the latter, and after a subsequent conversation with her, my guess was confirmed.

Basically, she was upset because she felt unfairly treated. In her mind, her rights had been violated, and she had suffered. We had taken her phone away, turned up the heat, and neglected to inform her of our true intentions that evening. Such an experience was unacceptable to her. Now, that might seem silly to you, but generally, she's not alone in the belief that the default of life should be one of comfort.

I've observed a relatively common struggle among students today—a pattern of intolerance of inconvenience and suffering. Now, I know this isn't true for everyone, of course. I have personally sat and cried with many young people who have known tremendous loss, heartache, pain, and trials. Many who suffer lean into it well, and wholeheartedly trust God as they endure the hardships he allows into their lives. But I've also seen young people avoid suffering, the path of least resistance prized above all else.

For example, I've noticed that many people today are often so terrified of confrontation that there is a tendency to often break off communication with someone entirely just to avoid conflict. I have witnessed and been tempted myself to "ghost someone" or stop returning text messages.[1] We don't want to suffer through anything remotely close to relational discomfort, so we simply avoid it. If discomfort or uneasiness (mild forms of suffering) can be sidestepped, we will usually dodge it.

And while some might read what I've just written and scoff at being singled out in this way as a conflict-avoidant student, the truth is this is a problem for most people, regardless of age. No one is really immune to backing away from hard times if given the choice. I know I generally opt for comfort and ease when I'm plotting out my day or thinking about my calendar commitments. My nature is to constantly bring life back to a state of personal comfort, and I'd be willing to bet your nature is the same. Why? Because we've been trained from birth to eliminate suffering from every part of our lives. Think about it—when we're hungry, we eat; when we're hot, we turn on the air conditioning; when we're uncomfortable with what we're wearing, we change clothes; when we have a headache, we take Tylenol. It's almost everything all the time!

Now, don't get me wrong here: the examples I just mentioned aren't intrinsically bad in and of themselves. However, it's easy to see we've grown accustomed to the normalcy of these comforts in our everyday existence. Little issues (such as turning on the air conditioning when we're uncomfortably hot, for example) can begin hardwiring us to immediately flee when any kind of suffering pops up in our lives. We can't put up with hardship for any significant amount of time because we've been trained to constantly purge it from our existence. My knee-jerk reaction to the heat is to lunge for the thermostat and cool my home down, and you can probably think of a similar example you have in your life when it comes to an intolerance of discomfort. No doubt you've reached for your phone in the midst of an uncomfortable environment or conversation just to ease the mild suffering of the moment by staring at your screen. Why? Because our phones make us feel better.

But if we are willing to push back on our reactive nature and walk for a time in the suffering, we can begin to identify with the beauty of Christ's suffering in ways we never would have before. In the past when we continually chose a life of comfort and ease, we missed out on opportunities to see Christ in deeper, more intimate ways. We were unable to commune with him and profoundly connect because we were so focused on ourselves. See, Jesus is our divine friend in the fires of life, bringing new significance to Isaiah 43:2, 5 when it says, "When you walk through the fire you shall not be burned, and the flame shall not consume you . . . Fear not, for I am with you."[2]

In the hard times of life, I've certainly asked the question, "Where are you, Jesus?" But if I'm honest, I've asked that question from an improper perspective—a self-centered perspective.

Nearly every time I ask that question, I'm really saying, "Lord, get me out of this situation because it's really hard and I don't want to suffer. Please just make my life easier so I can move on to my schedule, my needs, my desires, my purposes, my goals, my life!"

But the key thing I'm missing in my little self-absorbed tirades as I suffer is that my life isn't my own (1 Corinthians 6:19–20), and the trials I go through aren't unimportant distractions from my real life, they are a specific conduits of God's grace in my life to bring me closer in relationship with him, while shaping me more into the image of his Son.[3]

The Pain in My Behind

For much of my life, I've been a runner. Back in middle school, I was a part of the long-distance track team. Notice I didn't say "competitive part." I participated on the team, and that was good enough for me. I was active, it helped me connect with other kids socially, and I enjoyed doing something other than academics while at school. Plus I only weighed about 87 pounds, so taking part in a sport that requires no physical contact with another human being is a great one when you're roughly the size of a baby Hobbit.

As I moved on into my high school years, I naturally continued running on both the track team, and then the cross-country team. I loved it for many reasons and was thankful for those chapters in my life, but when I reached college age, I discontinued my running "adventures" and didn't really pick them back up again until I got married almost a decade later. My wife and I have enjoyed running together on several occasions, and we both even entered a few long-distance races in the greater Philadelphia area where we now live.

One such race was the Broad Street Run—a ten-mile race through the heart of central Philadelphia that started as a straight shot from the northern part of the city and ended near the sports stadiums where the Flyers, Eagles, and Phillies play. We both trained hard for the race and were in great shape once the starting gun went off.

Despite the drizzling rain during the majority of the race that morning, my wife and I both had a great experience running in it, and even finished with running times we could both be happy telling other people about. In the days following, we did a few "cool down" runs to make sure our bodies adjusted appropriately because we weren't on the training schedule anymore, and we even ran sporadically to stay in shape as springtime ended and the summer approached.

But about fourteen days after my wife and I ran the Broad Street Run, I started to feel this stabbing pain in my right leg that started up in the middle of my right-side lower back and extended all the way down the back of my leg to the middle of my right calf muscle. The pain was sharp in some places on my leg/upper thigh, and throbbing enough in other places to make me uncomfortable in nearly any position I tried to get in while standing or sitting. Sometimes it felt better when I would wake up from sleep in the morning, but most of the time it was a steady stream of pain that cut into me on a consistent enough basis that made it impossible to ignore.

During those summer months after the Broad Street Run, I was away from home on a mission trip out of state, so I didn't have direct access to my family physician other than by phone. I called him and told him what my symptoms were, but without an in-office examination, it was going to be impossible to accurately diagnose what my specific issue was. I had to wait until I got home before I could get on the solution side of what was making my leg hurt so much. I gritted my teeth through much of those painful two months, and when the summer mission was over, I immediately went to go see my doctor.

After a series of tests, including numerous physical examinations, a blood sample, and an MRI, my doctor came to the conclusion that I had a bulging disc between my L5 and S1 vertebrae that was putting pressure on my sciatic nerve, causing the radiating pain from my lower back to the middle of my right leg. Apparently, the diagnosis was a common one for many people who were physically active like me, so he prescribed some anti-inflammatory medication and six to eight weeks of physical therapy in order to strengthen the core muscles around my spine and relieve some of that pressure on my sciatic nerve. We hoped that would do the trick and eliminate the pain that acted as a constant irritation in my daily life . . . but it didn't.

Eight weeks of physical therapy sessions came and went, and the pain still remained. As a fellow dedicated follower of Jesus, my doctor prayed for me during my routine appointments and remained optimistic as we moved on to another potential solution. He recommended injections that would localize the medication to that specific area in my back and possibly make the pain subside. Despite my irrational fear of needles, I agreed and trusted that this was going to be the best solution for me.

But it wasn't. In fact, during the second injection procedure, the specialist working on me accidentally clipped the nerve in my back, causing it to spasm. That error put me in the most excruciating pain I've ever experienced for two solid days. I was miserable. I remember one night leaning against the wall in my bathroom with my head buried in the towels that hung from the rack and crying uncontrollably because I was in so much pain.

The following months brought more potential solutions, but no relief. I tried seeing a chiropractor, an orthopedic specialist, a neurosurgeon, and even an acupuncturist. Nothing helped. I discussed lower back surgery with the neurosurgeon in our meeting together, but after an examination of my most recent MRI, he told me he didn't see anything in the images that would warrant major surgery. Plus, there were no guarantees it would be successful and take away my pain anyway.

Many failed attempts to restore my health and nearly a decade later, I continue to live with daily chronic pain. It has been the greatest test of endurance, patience, and waiting I have ever had to go through. But through my discouragement over these many years, God has revealed himself to me in ways I never would have been able to see had I not suffered.

In this long haul, I've learned that I have spent my entire life desiring to "cross the finish line" of suffering or trials. I've been enlightened to my own selfish questioning of God with examples like, "When is this going to be over?" and "Where's the light at the end of the tunnel?" But the reality I need to face with my pain is that there might not be a finish line in all of this for me in this life (before heaven). And if there isn't, what good is there in constantly focusing on when it will be done if it may never end?

Eventually, God led me to specific verses like Psalm 27:14, which says, "Wait for the LORD; be strong, and let your heart take courage; wait for the LORD!"

And then an epiphany came to me one day. I realized I shouldn't spend my life looking for the finish line of this trial by wanting my suffering to end quicker so I could get through it and be done. I shouldn't look to the end, but to the side, where I will see Jesus alongside me in this race, with understanding in his eyes, throughout every single stride. When I came to that realization, I was able to pray that I would be so enamored with the Lord, I wouldn't even dwell on getting things over with rapidly, crossing the finish line of pain. I prayed I would be able to patiently walk through the pain, knowing my Savior understands and walks right next to me as he leads me into joy because ultimately, it is all for my good.

Cold Comfort

I know it can be unbearably difficult to understand some of the bitter realities in life, and I don't at all mean to downplay any legitimate hurt you might be going through right now by suggesting all of our trials are really God's goodness in disguise. I have friends who have lost their parents to cancer, lost their children in car accidents, seen their businesses crumble and financially collapse, gone through excruciating physical torment, and been in a place of such despair that they've looked at me through tears and screamed, "Why would God allow this? Where is Jesus in this misery?"

My response in those moments has not been to coldly quote Romans 8:28 and make up some idea that it's all going to be great someday. That would be a cruel way to respond in the midst of someone's suffering. Usually I just cry alongside them and tell them I don't know, because sometimes "I don't know" is the best answer one can give to someone in the depths of despair.

Evil is real. Sin is real. This world is significantly broken, and sometimes those realities cross our paths in very real ways that bring torment to our lives. Sometimes we have the benefit of hindsight and we're able to understand why God allowed certain things to happen, and other times we'll never know the reasons why things happened the way they did for us because the whole thing is a huge mystery.

What I do know is God was willing to sacrifice his own Son to be in relationship with me, and that fact alone will always be evidence enough to support the truth that God is good and he loves me. My circumstantial evidence might tell a different story, but I must never allow my personal experiences to negate the truth of Scripture. Assigning blame or numbing the pain in your choice of personal vice does nothing but walk us backward or stall us out.

Plain Biblical Evidence

When Jesus heard from afar that his friend Lazarus was deathly ill in John 11, he intentionally stayed two days longer in the place where he was and didn't rush to his friend's aide. The text says he did this because it was for the glory of God and also because he loved Lazarus and Lazarus's two sisters, Mary and Martha (John 11:4–6). I always thought it was odd that Jesus let Lazarus die and his sisters suffer *because* he loved them. It used to seem counterintuitive to me that he loved them and simultaneously ushered deep, intentional hurt into their lives.

But then my life got turned upside down because of my chronic back and leg pain, and the theory of suffering became a real-world experience for me. In the height of my misery, I would pore over texts in the Bible, hunting for evidence that Jesus wasn't an absentee landlord in my life. Eventually I came upon this story in the gospel of John, and was reminded of what happened to this group of siblings and how Christ interacted with them during something so impossibly difficult as death.

I read that he allowed it to happen so the Son of Man (Jesus himself) would be glorified through it, and he waited on purpose an extra two days because he loved Lazarus and his sisters. But what I neglected to remember is what happened later in verses 33–36:

> When Jesus saw her weeping, and the Jews who had come with her also weeping, he was *deeply moved* in his spirit and *greatly troubled*. And he said, "Where have you laid him?" They said to him, "Lord, come and see." *Jesus wept.* So the Jews said, "See how he loved him!" (John 11:33–36, my emphasis added)

Yes, Jesus allowed Lazarus's death to happen because of his love for them, but do you see how he was also present in their lives as they suffered? The text says Jesus "was deeply moved" and "greatly troubled." It also says he wept with them. He was emotionally shaken even though he knew full well that he was about to raise their brother from the dead. He cried with them in the moment, knowing joy was in their immediate future. That might seem strange, but it's only odd if there's no purpose behind the relationship. Jesus obviously cared and related to everything Mary and Martha were going through because the process is just as important as the final outcome—if not more so.

Our God isn't watching our misery from afar. He is right there in it with us, grieving with us, hurting with us, weeping with us just as he was all those years ago with Mary and Martha. God cares about us. The life, death, and resurrection of Christ proves that beyond any doubt, so let's place our trust in him even when we can't understand the "why" in any given suffering situation.

He Gets It

If suffering was a defining characteristic of Jesus's life on earth, it stands to reason that if we want to be more Christlike, we will inevitably suffer. The answer to the question, *Where is Jesus when I suffer?* is obviously, *He's right beside you.* Jesus gets it. He personally understands what it means to be isolated, persecuted, rejected, unloved, and deeply hurt. He is with you in hard times, both small and big.

When that friend of yours suddenly turns on you and doesn't want to hang out anymore? That's God's grace, and he understands your suffering. When you don't make it into your first-choice school after praying and praying that you'll get in? That's God's grace too. When your boyfriend or girlfriend dumps you via text message without as much as a follow-up explanation? That's God's grace and protection. When that so-labeled "easy" class becomes the bane of your existence because there's so much homework? That's God's grace. When you don't get the callback for the job interview you were certain you slam dunked? That's God's grace. Or to put it in another, more catchy way: every rejection is God's protection.[4]

Now, let me pause here for the sake of clarity. Will you be sinned against in some of these suffering situations? Of course, and I'm not saying that's okay. But ultimately, it's not the main point because God can and will use the sin of others to accomplish his purposes in your life.[5] Really, our perspective should not be to point out who or what is to blame when we suffer, but to seek the Lord and trust that he is in control, showering us in his grace as we walk with him.

And sometimes that can feel really odd, because my natural reaction to pain and suffering is certainly not, "Wow! God is extending so much grace to me right now!" But if he is sovereign (and he is), and I walk by faith as I trust in the promises of Scripture, reminding myself that he loves me (which we've already talked about in a previous chapter), every smooth surface and every bump in the road is a conduit of God's grace. Every good and perfect gift is from him (James 1:17), and every rejection is God's protection.

Pinned Down

When my first daughter was a little over two years old, she accidentally scratched her cornea in the middle of the night while she was sleeping. As a result, my wife and I took her to the hospital, and it was determined that she needed to get a scan on her eyeball after special eye drops were administered. The doctor looked at me and said my wife and I would have to physically pin my daughter down by her shoulders so the drops could be put in her eye correctly, and they'd be able to diagnose the severity of the scratch. For her good, we agreed that the procedure needed to happen, but it's kind of difficult to explain the complexity of a situation like that to a toddler. Simply put, my daughter didn't want anything put in her eye and her opinion was expressed clearly via her writhing body and ear-piercing shrieks.

I'll never forget that morning, because the screams of my little girl still echo in my mind when I remember that procedure. I had to hold my baby girl down and stop her little squirming head from moving while the nurse put drops in her eye. She screeched in terror unlike anything I'd ever heard before, and I cried as I saw it all happening up close. I knew it was for her good, and I knew her two-year-old mind couldn't understand what was happening to her, so I made the call to hold her down because I dearly loved and cared about the well-being of my daughter in spite of her ignorance.

I'm sure she must have been wondering why her mommy and daddy would be a part of something so traumatic. I'm sure she couldn't comprehend why her parents were accomplices in what was happening to her. We pinned her down and she had no idea why. But the procedure helped confirm the diagnosis, she got the medicine she needed, and Rachael and I would do it all over again if we had to because it was for her good.

I often remind myself of this story when I'm tempted to ask where Jesus might be during the hardship of life. I'm sure, like me, you're quick to point the finger at God and accuse him of being absent in your life when the trials roll over you. But the reality is just the opposite of our angry accusations. He is quite present in the suffering. In fact, the trials we may be unable to comprehend might be the very means by which he chooses to bless us with his loving grace. When we blame God or numb ourselves with habitual phone screen gazing, we're missing out on deeper connection and growth with our Maker.

To push away the hurt when God Almighty is trying to draw closer to us is truly sad. Ignoring his loving care while he wants to teach us through a vehicle as powerful as suffering neglects his tenderness even when that tenderness might feel like sandpaper to our soul. Embrace the suffering. Learn from it and grow wiser because of it. In doing so, you'll see more and more detail revealed about the Savior—our suffering servant, Jesus Christ.

Where Is Jesus in the Hard Times?—Reflection Questions
1. In what ways are you constantly trying to bring your life back to a state of comfort?

2. Who or what have you been tempted to blame when you suffer? How can you turn those accusations into trusting the Lord when hard times come?

3. How can you develop a gospel-centered approach to suffering when it seems impossible to do so?

Conclusion

When I first arrived on campus my freshman year of college, I had no clue about anything in my new environment. In high school, I never had the chance to visit and tour my university, and earlier that summer after graduation, I had missed freshman orientation. This was before the advent of smartphones, and I didn't have a personal computer, so when I arrived at school as a nervous eighteen-year-old kid, it was the Saturday before classes started and I was probably the most ignorant freshman moving into the dorms.

By God's grace, my randomly assigned roommate was a sophomore, and he agreed to show me the buildings where my classes would be on Monday so I didn't wander the campus like an aimless New York City tourist, asking every person I saw for directions. After my classes on Monday, I took the time to learn where my Tuesday/Thursday classes would be, and on that hot and humid day as I searched, I vividly remember thinking that I was in *way* over my head.

Literally everything on that college campus was new to me. I had no idea what to do or what to expect. It was all a mystery: how to get to a quiet place to study, how to check out a book at the library, how to find the soft-serve ice cream machine at the dining hall, and how to function on my own without my parents' supervision.

Yet like most every other college freshman, I learned in time.

Life in the modern age is unexplored territory. New gadgets, new complications, new apps, and new ideas about how to connect the world will keep washing over the human race until Jesus himself returns. It's inevitable, and kind of terrifying when you think about it. We simply don't know what to expect.

And with the natural pressure points that arrive as a direct result of living in this modern age as a follower of Jesus Christ, there comes tremendous opportunity to walk with God in the midst of the stress, trials, and tension. Yes, your challenges as a college student today are much more nuanced than the generations who came before you, but with those challenges come new opportunities to set the bar high in the pursuit of his glory through your life. We have the means to push back darkness in exciting ways—ways that enrich our walks with the Lord and take the gospel to the ends of the earth. Modernity has granted us that convenience via technology, and it's thrilling to live in a time where God's Word and his gospel message is so easily accessible.

Our Constant

The challenges we face are familiar—anxiety, control, relationship problems, insecurity, complicated friendships, patience, commitment, and so on—but all those pressure points get turned on their head as we wrestle with them in the context of our current culture. Yes, there is nothing new under the sun (Ecclesiastes 1:9), but our problems become more complex when filtered through today's lens. And although we as God's people grapple with modernity's unique issues, the solution to our trouble remains the same. Scripture says, "Jesus Christ is the same yesterday and today and forever" (Hebrews 13:8).

Sure, you may have seen this verse cross-stitched onto a pillow at your grandmother's house, but that doesn't change the fact that it is enormously significant for us. Yesterday. Today. Forever on into the future. Jesus has been and always will be the immovable, unshakable constant on which we will eternally rely. The good news of his perfect life, his sacrificial death on our behalf, and his ultimate victory over the grave is still 100 percent relevant to the issues we all deal with every day in our fast-paced culture.

The gospel is the only true solution to our struggles. Cling to it in times of sadness, heartache, loneliness, hurt, and confusion. Cling to it in times of jubilation, zeal, comfort, fulfillment, exhilaration, and success. We need the gospel when things are horrible and we need the gospel when things are wonderful. He is the ultimate solution, regardless of the pressures you may be facing.

He is the Alpha and the Omega, the beginning and the end (Revelation 22:13). He is before all things, and in him all things hold together (Colossians 1:17). Nothing and no one will ever love you the way he does. Remember this as you struggle with the pressure points of life. It will make the experience worth it, because regardless of the outcome, it's an experience *with him*.

Acknowledgments

When average people win the lottery, they become wealthy in terms of dollars and cents. I hit the lottery, but I won something more valuable than money—I won the heart of my exceptional wife, Rachael. I can't believe you got suckered into spending the rest of your life with me, Rach. Thank you for encouraging me and loving Jesus first. I want to be like you when I grow up.

~ ~ ~

Thank you to the wise men in my life who have raised the bar for me over the years and pushed me to walk closely with Christ as a biblical man. Many of your words and ideas have shaped the way I think and communicate. I'm thinking specifically of Rick James, Dan Flynn, Roger Hershey, Dave Broadwell, Tim Henderson, Mike Carnuccio, and Paul Tripp. Thank you for spending your lives pouring into others like me. The world is not worthy of godly men like you.

~ ~ ~

Finally, I want to acknowledge some of my cheerleaders who have encouraged me in my writing over the years and opened doors, windows, and egresses for me. My friend Matt Smethurst, my coworker and friend Heather Holleman, and my Gas Bat partners for life: Andy Allan, Karl Armentrout, Tom Flack, and John Boggs.

Notes

Introduction

1. McDool, Powell, Roberts, and Taylor, *Social Media Use and Children's Wellbeing*, IZA Labor Institute of Economics, IZA DP No. 10412, http://ftp.iza.org/dp10412.pdf, December 2016, 3, accessed April 17, 2018.

2. "My Hope Is Built on Nothing Less," Edward Mote, 1834.

Section 1: The Pressure of Purpose

1: Does God Even Like Me?

1. Referencing Romans 8:1.

2. The rhetoric for Jesus suffering to be with us is found in Timothy Keller's *Walking with God through Pain and Suffering* (New York: Dutton, 2013), 234.

2: How Do I Decide My Life's Direction?

1. *The NAS New Testament Greek Lexicon.* http://www.biblestudy tools.com/lexicons/greek/nas/kaleo.html, accessed April 17, 2018.

3: What Does God Want Me to Do?

1. The phrasing of this example and a few others in this chapter were taken from a talk by Roger Hershey, and can also be found in his

book, *The Finishers*, by Roger Hershey and Jason Weimer (Orlando, FL: Cru Press, 2011).

2. Ibid.

4: What Does God Want from Me?

1. My wife and I don't necessarily agree with everything in the book, but this principle can be found in *Don't Make Me Count to Three* by Ginger Hubbard (Wapwallopen, PA: Shepherd Press, 2004).

5: How Do I Handle the Void?

1. From the Twitter feed of Francis Flood, twitter.com/ImSoFrancis, accessed April 17, 2018.

2. In 1670, Blaise Pascal published *Pensées*, which was a defense of the Christian religion. It was published after his death in 1662. In that book, he has a quote that reads, "What else does this craving, and this helplessness, proclaim but that there was once in man a true happiness, of which all that now remains is the empty print and trace? This he tries in vain to fill with everything around him, seeking in things that are not there the help he cannot find in those that are, though none can help, since this infinite abyss can be filled only with an infinite and immutable object; in other words, by God himself" (*Pensées VII*, 425). Since then, the concept has taken on a life of its own and the phrase "God-shaped hole" or "vacuum" has become a close approximation of the concept, and found throughout many Christian circles.

3. Timothy Keller, *Shaped by the Gospel* (Grand Rapids, MI: Zondervan, 2016), 127.

Section 2: The Pressure of Relationships

6: The Physicality of Modern Romance

1. Andrew Byers, *TheoMedia: The Media of God and the Digital Age* (Eugene, OR: Cascade Books, 2013).

7: The Ambiguity of Modern Romance

1. Christopher Hudspeth, *18 Ugly Truths About Modern Dating That You Have to Deal With*, https://thoughtcatalog.com/christopher-hudspeth/2014/04/18-ugly-truths-about-modern-dating-that-you-have-to-deal-with/, accessed April 17, 2018.

2. J. K. Rowling, *Harry Potter and the Goblet of Fire* (New York: Scholastic Press, 2000), 628.

8: Wrestling with Parental Guidance

1. Jaquelle Crowe, *This Changes Everything* (Wheaton, IL: Crossway, 2017), 135–36.

2. Ibid., 137.

9: Is True Friendship Possible?

1. C. S. Lewis, *The Four Loves* (London: Geoffrey Bles, 1960), 94.

2. Ralph Waldo Emerson, *Essays: First Series, Friendship* (1841).

3. Walter Winchell's syndicated newspaper column, Jimmy Nelson, mid-January, 1955.

10: Cultural Consumerism and Connecting with Community

1. Sam Allberry, *Why Bother with Church?* (Surrey, UK: The Good Book Company, 2016), 9.

2. Byron Straughn, *Like Families and Soccer Teams*, 9Marks Journal, March-April Issue, 2011.

3. *How to Go Church Shopping*, http://www.relevantmagazine.com/god/church/features/18261-church-shopping, published September 17, 2009, accessed April 17, 2018.

11: FOMO (Fear of Missing Out)

1. https://www.ted.com/talks/sherry_turkle_alone_together?language=en, accessed April 17, 2018.

2. Dr. John M. Grohol, Psy.D., *FOMO Addiction: The Fear of Missing Out*, http://psychcentral.com/blog/archives/2011/04/14/fomo-addiction-the-fear-of-missing-out/, accessed April 17, 2018.

3. Dr. John M. Grohol, Psy.D., *FOMO Addiction: The Fear of Missing Out*, http://psychcentral.com/blog/archives/2011/04/14/fomo-addiction-the-fear-of-missing-out/, accessed April 17, 2018.

4. From a sermon by Matt Chandler on fear and anxiety, given at The Village Church. http://thevillagechurch.net/resources/sermons/detail/sanctification-examining-fear-and-anxiety, accessed April 17, 2018.

12: Dealing with Enemies

1. D. A. Carson, *Love in Hard Places* (Wheaton, IL: Crossway, 2002), 61.

2. Timothy Keller, *Serving Each Other Through Forgiveness and Reconciliation*, from an article that first appeared in The Gospel and Life conferences of 2004 and 2005.

Section 3: The Pressure Because of Difficulty

13: Immediate Success and Depth of Character

1. Interview with Simon Sinek by London Real, *Self-Esteem, Gratification, and Addiction,* https://www.youtube.com/watch?v=PMEqLzWrMIo, accessed April 17, 2018.

2. Daniel Dunlap, *Living in the Tension,* http://www.ligonier.org/learn/articles/living-in-the-tension/, accessed April 17, 2018.

14: Spiritual Warfare

1. From the Twitter feed of Garrett Kell, https://twitter.com/pastorjgkell/status/973915342115352576, accessed April 17, 2018.

15: Peer Evaluation

1. Tony Reinke, *Should Teens Own Smartphones?,* October 16, 2017, https://www.desiringgod.org/articles/should-teens-own-smartphones, accessed April 17, 2018.

2. ABC News, *Excessive Cell Phone Use May Cause Anxiety, Experts Warn,* July 28, 2017, http://abcnews.go.com/Lifestyle/excessive-cellphone-anxiety-experts-warn/story?id=48842476, accessed April 17, 2018.

16: Where Is Jesus in the Hard Times?

1. This idea was shared in an interview with Simon Sinek by London Real, *Self-Esteem, Gratification, and Addiction,* https://www.youtube.com/watch?v=PMEqLzWrMIo, accessed April 17, 2018.

2. A few ideas sparked by reading Timothy Keller's *Walking with God through Pain and Suffering* (New York: Dutton, 2013), 232–36.

3. The wise words of Paul David Tripp helped me more deeply understand suffering as a means of receiving God's grace. For further reference, I recommend his daily devotional, *New Morning Mercies* (Wheaton, IL: Crossway, 2014).

4. A friend and fellow author, Heather Holleman, says this is her family's motto.

5. See Joseph's story in Genesis 37–50, culminating in Genesis 50:20, and also how Jonah's sinful rebellion against God's specific commands led to the salvation of the pagan mariners in Jonah 1.